To Ralph & Sue

Very best wishes.

Sid Davis

2-13-89

Delta
Air Lines

Debunking the Myth

Delta
Air Lines

Debunking the Myth

Sidney F. Davis

PEACHTREE PUBLISHERS, LTD.

Atlanta • *Memphis*

Published by
PEACHTREE PUBLISHERS, LTD.
494 Armour Circle, NE
Atlanta, Georgia 30324

Manufactured in the United States of America

10 9 8 7 6 5 4 3 2 1

Cover design by Phil Scopp

Library of Congress Catalog Card Number 88-61456

ISBN 0-934601-55-0

To Susie

"The only certainty in
life—and in corporate life, too—
is that there is none."
—Malcolm Forbes

CONTENTS

PREFACE

In February of 1967, when I joined Delta Air Line's staff as the junior member of a staff comprised of four corporate attorneys, I felt that I had a wonderful opportunity to combine the law and my first love, aviation. Although I had been in private practice after law school and had found that practice rewarding, I had always regretted that my earlier experience as a Navy pilot had not yet been utilized in my legal career. So when the call from Delta came, it seemed clear to me that the psychic income from being involved with aircraft again would be incalculable and that my quest for professional fulfillment could be more dynamically realized in this energetic company.

Time has proven me right. Not only did my participation in and eventual leadership of the Delta negotiation team in mega-million dollar airplane contracts, including involvement in all of the commercial aspects of the company, bring professional satisfaction and accomplishment, but my role in the legal department at Delta during those 13 years offered the kinds of opportunities that most young commercial lawyers only dream about.

In those early days of my involvement with Delta, the company was a self-starting institution where professionals could challenge themselves and test their limits for growth. By the time I left Delta in 1979 to become vice president and general counsel of Springs Industries, Inc., another *Fortune* 500 industrial company, I had risen to become Delta's number two lawyer, vice president and assistant general counsel of a staff which had grown from four to 20 during my tenure. And when, toward the end of that 13-year period it seemed all that earlier dynamism had evaporated—for me it was time to move on.

Since I left Delta, I have remained a student of the airline business and kept close contact within the industry in general and at Delta in particular. The book I planned to write was to contain an appraisal of Delta's fortunes since deregulation. I did not begin this book with any preconceived notions; indeed, while I guessed that Delta had not fared well during this period, I had no idea what I might find.

Ultimately, the book I have written is not an optimistic one, as the findings do not make the kind of story the Delta public relations department would appreciate. I thought long and hard before I released this book for publication, and on more than one occasion considered abandoning the project altogether. No one likes to write a negative book, but I could not bring myself to paint an optimistic face upon what I have come to see as Delta's failure to come to grips with deregulation.

This book is a payment for a debt I owe to a company that was an important part of my past. It is payment for a debt I owe to many fine people who are held back and stifled by conditions at Delta, people who are frustrated by their inability to reach their potential and who are therefore unable to make their maximum contributions to the company.

When people found out that I was writing a book on Delta, their first question was: "Why are you writing it?" The second was usually "What is there to say about Delta, it's a great company?" In most cases, those were not just queries. There was nearly always a tone of apprehension—if not downright suspicion—in their voices, as if they were really asking why someone who had a very successful career with the company should undertake an analysis of Delta.

I have written this book to say that the "emperor has no clothes," to expunge the illusion that Delta is OK. Fact is Delta is *not* OK. Fact is Delta no longer deserves the reputation that it is financially impregnable and can endure and prosper in the worst of times. Fact is Delta is in need of strong medicine if it is to survive over the long term. During the brief but sharp recession of the early 1980s Delta was unable to cope with external factors. As a result, during this period, Delta turned in a few years of poor earnings and one year of dramatic losses. In the fiscal year ending June 30, 1988, Delta's figures show that its operating expenses increased more than its operating income from the prior year. This poor showing occurred notwithstanding strong demands for its services, higher air fares through the summer of 1988 and the debilitation of its major competitor, Eastern.

In writing this book, I had several choices. I could write a scholarly book, cool and distanced. But that book would have been easily dismissed, lost on the lists of business texts. Or I could write a hard-hitting book with a gloves-off style that would be controversial, demanding, talked about. That I chose the last option was necessary if anything is to be done about Delta.

Delta is the principal air carrier in Atlanta, serving all major cities in the United States and several foreign cities. It would be catastrophic for Atlanta in particular and for the Southeast in general if Delta were to join Eastern on the industrial scrap heap. Because these two ailing companies control roughly 90 percent of the air traffic in and out of Atlanta, such a result could prove ruinous to Atlanta with its ambitious plans for the future.

Atlanta cannot remain complacent about Delta. It cannot afford to turn a blind eye to Delta's weaknesses. If we are to have a strong airline based in Atlanta, then we have to exert pressure to insist on competitive excellence and managerial prowess. That means we have to care how Delta handles its problems and speak out loudly when it handles them poorly.

I expect this to prove a thankless project, as I am reasonably confident that Delta's bunker mentality will permit none. Nevertheless, Delta is a cherished Atlanta institution, and few cherish her more than I who have prospered greatly in her service. It is my hope that in days and weeks ahead we will have time to consider these problems, that Delta will take time to listen to my argument, and that someone somewhere will encourage the kind of changes that need to be undertaken for Delta to regain its footing and continue as a strong and responsible company.

Notes From the Author

As befits a public company, facts, figures and pertinent information are necessarily in the public domain and, as such, available as public information. Statistical data in this book were taken from information compiled and furnished by the airlines to the Department of Transportation. In some cases, it is dated on a trailing 12-month basis. The data were collected by such firms as The Boeing Company and a number of airline consulting firms throughout the United States. To that end, the author wishes to acknowledge with thanks the good assistance of Airline Economics, Inc., in Washington, D.C., for compiling the data used herein to make the analyses in all of the essential areas not directly related to balance sheets or profit-and-loss statements, such as yields, market shares, computerized reservations systems and traffic figures.

Also, the author wishes to thank BCI Consulting Group of Atlanta, an independent consulting firm that assisted in the travel agency surveys and also performed the analysis, in conjunction with a certified public accounting firm, of the earnings performance of Delta, using Delta's annual reports to stockholders.

The assistance of these firms has been invaluable and, hopefully, establishes credibility with the reader as to the validity of the premises set forth in such analyses.

The author wishes to acknowledge, with special thanks, Roger Easson for his contribution to the preparation of this book.

Special thanks, too, to Nancy Wood, my secretary. Nancy's dedication and enthusiasm saw me through; she helped write the book.

PROLOGUE

Delta.
The name of the fourth letter in the Greek alphabet.
A triangular tract of alluvial land formed at the mouth of a river.

To Southerners, the word "Delta" literally means the land extending south from Memphis to the Gulf of Mexico—where the ancient riverbed of the wandering Mississippi has created some of the richest farm land in the American South.

Culturally, the word means something far more profound, it is intrinsic to a Southern mystique. The Delta is a land of postcard scenes, of cotton fields and of historic plantations from which the image makers draw their visions of the South. It is a land of the blues and jazz in which the poor give voice to their sufferings and their joys. The Delta gave us Elvis and B.B. King and Jimmy Swaggart. It is a land of Cajun tradition and Napoleonic legal codes, a land torn by intense conflicts called Shiloh and Vicksburg, intensities carefully bred into the youth by accumulated memories of a conquered people. As legend has it, the Delta begins in the lobby of the Peabody Hotel in downtown Memphis, a city some call "the biggest town in Mississippi."

It is appropriate, therefore, that the airline which had its origins in the Louisiana side of the Mississippi Delta, and that has prospered as the South has prospered should be named "Delta." For over 60 years, during nearly 50 of which the airline has been based in Atlanta, Delta has built its fortress-like office complex and has garnered the reputation

1

of being a service-oriented Southern airline with all the graciousness the term "southern hospitality" implies. It is no wonder, then, that to this airline there clings an intense southern pride, a pride provoked by the name and, at one time, a pride richly deserved.

The great era of Delta's origins and growth ended with the death in late 1966 of C.E. Woolman, the founder and paternalistic master of the company. To this day, everyone at the senior management level knew Mr. Woolman and had worked for him either directly or indirectly with the one exception of Thomas Roeck, the former chief financial officer of Western Airlines who has recently been named to the same post at Delta. Part of the legacy Delta inherited from Mr. Woolman was the distinct impression that it was a very great privilege to work for Delta.

Today, this great and wonderful family of over 50,000 souls is quartered in a complex of red brick buildings near the airport, which remains carefully isolated from the public. When Delta moved to Atlanta in the early 1940s, however, headquarters were in a modest brick building added on to the back of an old hangar that served the original Atlanta airport. For many years it was a source of pride to Delta executives to show their austere offices to the financial press and contrast them with the plush offices of Pan American on Park Avenue in New York City.

Vestiges of this virtuous primitivism still cling to the offices in the old complex: even today, all offices have linoleum. The only exceptions are the carpeted offices of assistant vice presidents and higher-ranking officers. When an office is vacated by a rug-bearing officer and is slated to be subsequently occupied by a member of lower order the rug is unceremoniously pulled up and the linoleum restored. Even as newer buildings have been added to the complex, this premise has been retained.

During the decade of the 70s, two totally unrelated events had a profound impact on Delta. In my opinion these two events have caused the company to deviate from a course of being consistently the most financially strong and

innovative airline in the industry to one that seems unsure
of how to chart its course for the future.

The first of these events was the ascension to the
chairmanship of the board of Tom Beebe in 1970. While it is
difficult to find a contribution that Beebe personally made to
the company during his tenure, he indelibly set the stage for
the management team that will govern the company well
into the 21st century. Beebe, carrying the famous Delta
promotion from within policy to its extreme, ensured the
ascension of Ron Allen to the chairmanship over a whole
generation of managers. The result had a stultifying effect
on a group of senior managers who have retired or will be
retiring over the next few years and it moved to center stage
at a critical time in Delta's history a chief executive officer
who lacks the breadth of background and the experience, in
my opinion, to be a successful competitor in this environment where airlines continue to fumble through the chaos
created by the Airline Deregulation Act of 1978.

The Airline Deregulation Act is the second event that
has influenced Delta profoundly. While Delta entered
deregulation with a strong balance sheet, it has demonstrated in the ten years of deregulation that it lacks the
wherewithal to cope with the laissez faire of the marketplace. The current generation of senior managers at Delta
began their careers at Delta before deregulation and I believe
the evidence suggests that they have not adapted well to the
changes that have come with deregulation.

Thus, of the two events described above, deregulation
clearly is the most important. Some consumers and some
representatives of congress are demanding a return to regulation of the airline industry. No matter what kind of
statutes are enacted, the industry can never return to the
halcyon days pre-1978. It is important, therefore, to understand the origins of deregulation and the effect it has had
not only on Delta, but the industry at large. That is why the
first chapter of this book is devoted to a brief overview of
the industry pre and post deregulation. An understanding
of the attitudes and thinking of government during the later
part of President Ford's and early part of President Carter's

administrations provides useful insight to understanding the problems that are currently plaguing the airline industry.

—————— Chapter One ——————

Notes for Teaching AMTRAK to Fly

"Business is like sex. When it's good,
It's very good. When it's not so good,
It's still good."
—George Katona

The Origins of Regulation

Historically, regulation of the airline industry by the U.S. Government was a by-product of the U.S. Postal Service's desire to encourage the delivery of mail by air. To nurture this more rapid delivery method within the fledgling commercial airline industry, the government established regulations to subsidize air mail routes. With the evolution of the Douglas DC-2 and, especially, the DC-3, which could provide overnight transcontinental air service, Congress enacted the Civil Aeronautics Act of 1938 in order to create a new federal agency—the Civil Aeronautics Authority, later called the Civil Aeronautics Board [CAB]—which would dispense routes and establish rates for passenger fares and freight carriage. To make a long and very complex story simple, suffice it to say that after World War II the system had become cumbersome because the CAB was charged with all aspects of commercial aviation in the United States.[1]

Ultimately, when Congress was forced to recognize that the enormous complexity of the airline and airways system required major revision of the regulatory system, it passed the Federal Aviation Act of 1958. This act established a separate agency, the Federal Aviation Administration [FAA], which was charged with the regulation of airways systems and safety for all non-military aviation in the United States. The CAB remained the paternalisic godfather for the dispensing of rate and route authority to the airlines.

When deregulation was proposed in 1977, its stated intention was to provide free or automatic entry into markets which had been dominated by only one or in some cases, two carriers. During the ensuing six-year phase-out of regulation, if an airline filed an application to enter a market dominated by another airline, the airline which was already providing air service to that market could oppose the application if it could demonstrate that granting the prospective entrant access would not be in the public interest. This was no small task. In theory, the competitive effect of deregulation was to make the airlines more competitive and more cost-efficient.

At the time deregulation was enacted in 1978, the airline industry was the highest-paid industry in the country. The assumption was, and it seemed a reasonable one at the time, that airline managements would react sensibly to automatic entry and not throw assets and resources into markets where there was already sufficient service competition. There were also expectations that the pricing of airline tickets would be approached realistically, giving carriers a modicum of profit in the pricing arena. As then-CAB chairman Alfred Kahn said, automatic entry "will permit carrier managements to act like adult businessmen rather than remain forever wards of the state."[2] Given the current fine mess some airlines find themselves in, one wonders what happened to all those "adult businessmen" Kahn was so optimistic would materialize to manage his vision of a brave new airline industry.

Unfortunately, as we know all too well, that message has been lost on the captains of the airline industry. Today, many airlines generally price their services below cost and yet at a higher rate than would have been permitted under the old system. Deregulation has not only brought reduced air service in this country, but has also created pricing which is both unprofitable to the industry and still higher than it would have been had regulation remained in place. While this sounds like an anomaly, it is an unhappy reality, primarily because of the disparity in expenses throughout the industry.

Unaccountably, Delta operates today as if it is still in a regulated environment. While the airline enjoys substantial revenues, it nevertheless endures relatively thin operating profits which would, in earlier days, have been thought unacceptable. Continental is a low-cost operator, but because it has leveraged its assets so astronomically, it has to charge some incremental fare differential to support its debt service alone. Would all of this have happened without deregulation? Probably not. The CAB, through its much-maligned, paternalistic authority to award rate increases and additional routes, insulated the airline industry from such external factors as recessions and the vagaries of fuel pricing. Perhaps most important, however, was the CAB's ability to insulate the industry from inadequate management.

The Beginnings of Deregulation

The quagmire that is U.S. airline deregulation began in 1978. The Airline Deregulation Act of that year permitted air carriers to select their markets independently of government intervention and allowed each carrier the discretion to establish its own price structures. The legislation was spawned by the unlikely alliance of former President Gerald Ford, Senator Edward Kennedy, Senator Howard Cannon, and then-President Jimmy Carter. The House and Senate began hearings in 1977, and the Act was finally passed and signed by President Carter in October of the following year.

The Airline Deregulation Act was enacted because Congress was persuaded that the industry functioned as a government-sanctioned cartel. In addition, Congress concluded that industry salaries were too high and that there was little incentive to control operating costs or prices charged to consumers. It had been standard practice of regulated airlines to fly large aircraft with many empty seats and, as a result, airline tickets carried higher than necessary prices—or so the reasoning went.

Sponsors of the legislation believed that deregulation would lead to a more competitive environment which would, in effect, create conditions causing the industry to function more efficiently. That is to say, at least in theory, that the industry would operate with lower costs and hence would charge lower prices to the consumer. An influential Brookings Institution study[3] convinced Congress that this would expand the volume of air travel by making air travel more accessible to a greater segment of society, and there was Executive Branch support as well. Frustrated in their efforts to liberalize the airline industry by the long-standing constraints of the Federal Aviation Act of 1958, the Ford Administration was only too happy to encourage deregulation legislation.

There was support within the CAB as well, particularly from those who has been experimental with some loosening up of the Board's charter rules and so conveyed to the President and the Congress the need for legislation. Otherwise, recalls one participant who remains a strong proponent of deregulation, "There would have been a real patchwork of mumbo jumbo that would not have done the air transportation system any good."

In 1976, the Democrats won the White House, and as deregulation proponents were gearing up for the legislation, President Carter appointed Alfred Kahn chairman of the CAB. Kahn, a former Cornell University economics professor and head of the New York State Public Service Commission, was mandated to achieve as much deregulation as possible within the framework of the existing Federal Aviation Act.

A proponent of deregulation, Kahn set out immediately to advise those carriers which sought additional route authority and additional rate increases that no airline was entitled to survive if it couldn't make it on its own. To calm the opponents of deregulation who feared the chaos which would result from the free entry of airlines into existing markets served by their competitors, Kahn dismissed the notion that following deregulation, airline executives would "... use automatic entry to commit mass hara-kiri, that they will just pour stockholders' money into stupid adventures."[4]

In a letter to Kahn, a lawyer for Continental Airlines argued that with automatic entry, "...we [Continental Airlines] would have to displace or push aside one or more incumbents in order to achieve a profitable operation on new routes and Continental would be beset by new competition from big and little [air]lines alike."

Kahn's reply was scathing. "I guess that what I have heard about the legendary Bob Six [Robert Six, Continental's colorful and aggressive chairman at the time] is really some PR man's concoctions."[5]

Expressing doubts that Continental would suffer, Kahn added, "If every other carrier ... will feast on Continental, does the public interest demand that we protect you?"[6]

Pundits of the day noted that no one had protected the Ford Motor Company from building its Edsel, so why should anyone continue to protect the cartel-like practices of the airlines, particularly the large trunk airlines?

So-called "trunk airlines" are the original 12 large airlines—including, for example, American, Delta and United, that were in operation in 1938 when the initial Civil Aeronautics Act was enacted by Congress. Smaller carriers were referred to as "regional," or "feeder," airlines. Today, as a result of deregulation, that distinction between trunk and feeder carriers has become blurred and, in some cases, non-existent.

At the time of deregulation, it was acknowledged, even by its proponents as well as by the investment community, that many small feeder-type and regional airlines would, in all likelihood, be forced out of business. It was also expected that some smaller cities could lose their air service altogether if deregulation were enacted. Noting that some locations, such as Panama City, Florida, might lose trunk-line service entirely, Dr. Julius Maldutis, Jr., a widely respected airline analyst for Salomon Brothers, said at the time, "You'll see more of an implosion than an explosion" if deregulation permitting automatic market entry were enacted.[7]

While Jimmy Carter is said to have called the Airline Deregulation Act of 1978 the best piece of domestic legislation in his administration, others were not so unequivocal. For example, in a speech by the late Secor Browne, a former CAB chairman, he prophesied with enormous insight that the enactment of the Deregulation Act of 1978 will mean all of us are facing a flying AMTRAK. In another speech, Tom Beebe, Delta's chairman and CEO, worried in public that deregulation will mean that we will be putting flying box-cars in the sky. But perhaps the best description of the deregulated environment came from a senior executive of Boeing who predicted, with Darwinian accuracy, "The only guys who'll survive are those who eat raw meat."[8]

Among the domestic trunk airlines, none opposed deregulation more than American, Delta and Eastern. Delta's senior vice president and general counsel, Richard Maurer, appeared before the Senate's Cannon Committee several times to argue for only minimal changes to the existing Federal Aviation Act and against sweeping new legislation. It was Maurer's view, one embraced by Delta's management, that the proposed Cannon-Kennedy Bill would be the wrack and ruin of the airline industry. As if to dismiss his own concern about Delta's fate in such a devastated post-regulation environment and hence provide the illusion of objectivity for his testimony, Maurer reminded the Committee that Delta's financial strength would permit it to adapt to any environment the airline industry might face.

In his testimony, Maurer counseled moderation by suggesting only a fine tuning of existing statutory authority and warned against the radical changes contained in the Cannon-Kennedy Bill. At no time did Maurer's proposal contemplate a new statutory system that would phase out the Civil Aeronautics Board and deregulate the industry in terms of pricing and market entry. In fact, Maurer proposed that the Departments of Transportation and Justice be allowed to decide whether the antitrust laws of the country were violated when one or more air carriers proposed to merge. After his Senate testimony, he was personally complimented by both Senators Cannon and Goldwater on the completeness, insight and thoroughness of his testimony. While the compliments were no doubt genuine, Maurer's comments unfortunately fell on deaf ears, for the Cannon-Kennedy Bill became legislation.

One of the things I remember vividly about my tenure at Delta was that no one in the company really believed that deregulation as envisioned by the Cannon-Kennedy bill would really ever become law. For a few years prior to the actual event, the company's annual reports to shareholders would carry in the chairman's message a vague and ominous threat that if deregulation was enacted, it would almost certainly be the demise of the air transportation industry in this country as it had been known for 40 years. It should surprise no one, then, that Delta was caught flat-footed by deregulation as Delta's top management by and large lacked familiarization with—and understanding of—the ramifications of deregulation. Delta was ill-prepared and ill-equipped for the event when it actually happened, and in many ways, that is still true today.

For example, in an article ghost written by Dick Maurer for chairman and CEO Tom Beebe, and published in the November 1977 issue of *Finance Magazine*, Maurer made an eloquent plea to the investment community at large to oppose the Cannon-Kennedy Bill because its enactment would cause financial havoc in the industry and dry up sources of capital investment—even for strong carriers like Delta. The article asserted that the existing statute was sufficiently flexible, and, as such, capable of adapting to changing conditions. No thought was given to how (or if!) the industry in general—and Delta in particular—would react to deregulation if it indeed became law.[9]

American Airlines was also a very strong opponent of deregulation. American's chairman, Albert Casey, went so far as to suggest to the Cannon Committee that not only was deregulation unwise but that further legislation was needed to protect the airline industry from itself in regulating schedules and fares. This unexpected retrograde advice prompted an incredulous Senator Cannon to present Mr. Casey the "Dinosaur of the Month" award.

Also an opponent of airline deregulation, Eastern barely survives today because of the major contraction the company is experiencing as a result of deregulation. Frank Borman, Eastern's chairman during the deregulation debate, reaped the whirlwind himself when the Texas Air purchase of Eastern in 1986 forced him into retirement. Borman had been unable to make peace with the Eastern machinists' union, headed by Eastern employee Charles Bryant, who successfully lobbied himself onto Eastern's board of directors and then badgered Borman from the board room to the hangar shops. Ironically, the employees of Eastern probably lament the exchange of the pre-deregulation devil they knew, for the deregulation devil they got: Frank Lorenzo.

One of the ironies of the deregulation debate was that Richard Ferris, the chairman of UAL, Inc., the holding company for United Airlines, was a strong proponent of deregulation. He said that United would not abandon any of its routes, even if competitors came into play as a result of deregulation, because he reportedly liked them all, and all their routes were very profitable. Ferris' logic was clear: He believed that United, then the largest air carrier in the free world, had very limited opportunities for expanded route development under a benevolent CAB. Without the paternalistic Board, United could capitalize on its large size to expand even further to maintain its dominance. Like Borman, Ferris is gone from his post, having failed in his efforts to turn his company into something for everybody in the travel business. In effect, they tired of a certain emphasis on hotels, rental cars and package vacations instead of regaining a troubled United's once-dominant position as the largest air carrier in the free world.

Effects of Deregulation

In the first four years of deregulation, 1978 through 1982, many outside factors influenced the process. These factors included sharp fuel price increases, a major recession in the U.S. economy, and the now-famous air traffic controllers' strike. Fuel price increases alone forced airline costs up 28 percent in 1980. This volatile economic landscape allowed the managers of the established trunk airlines relatively few, if any, options for flexibility as they prepared to take advantage of deregulation.

Such was not the case, however, with smaller carriers. By virtue of their lower labor costs and the lower fuel costs inherent in their fleet of smaller aircraft, these small carriers were able to march on the market preserves of bigger carriers. The result was that the original 12 large trunk airlines, including Delta, lost large shares of their markets, dropping as much as 10 to 12 percentage points. One large trunk carrier, Braniff, disappeared entirely in 1982, although it later resumed operations as a relatively small, fragile operator.

These smaller carriers, however, were like moths to the candle. Most of them were under-capitalized, and by 1984 a substantial number had gone out of business. Others had the good fortune to attract the attention and, subsequently, the sponsorship of the large trunk carriers. Atlantic Southeast Air Lines, for example, is a thriving small carrier that serves as Delta's connection to many of the small cities in the Southeast which Delta does not service directly. It serves cities such as Brunswick, Georgia, and others where medium to small-sized turbo-prop airliners are able to make profits. Delta's DC-9s, for example, show only marginal operating profits in these same markets. Such carriers have received cash infusions from trunks, like Delta, which have purchased equity positions of up to 20 percent of their ownership. By and large, however, the smaller carriers have gone by the wayside, and those which remain prosper or fail at the whim of their sponsor.

If they did nothing else, these smaller carriers played an important role by providing the bigger carriers with a dramatic lesson in the realities of deregulation. It quickly became obvious that any perceived slack in the marketplace was going to be taken up by a new and eager contender, although, as it turned out in most cases, the staying power of such contenders was relatively short-lived.

Given this early period of economic volatility in which the bigger carriers were largely unable to take advantage of the newly deregulated environment, we should really date deregulated competition among the airlines from 1983, since that is the point when the bloodbath began. From 1983 to October 1986, no fewer than 45 scheduled carriers went belly-up through bankruptcy, merger or acquisition.

In 1984, the industry began to experience greater operating profitability, albeit one which would prove ultimately unsustainable. In 1984, the industry set a record operating income of $2.4 billion, followed by a drop to $1.4 billion in 1985 and another $1.4 billion in 1986.

From a bottom-line perspective, "dismal" is perhaps the only word to describe the performance of the major airlines since deregulation. Indeed, the major airlines are not so major any more, since as a group they have been reduced to eight from 12 by mergers, consolidations or common ownership. Between 1978 and 1987, the remaining trunks as a group have posted impressive revenues of $313.8 billion; however, the industry's operating margin is only 2 percent or, said another way, the industry earns only two cents on the dollar.

P. Jackson Bell, the highly respected chief financial officer of USAir, reported in a speech to the Air Finance Conference in New York on April 18, 1988 that the total net income for the entire U.S. airline industry for the nine years of deregulation has been only enough to purchase four new Boeing B-747s. Bell also noted that the airline industry cost structure now bears an embedded annual interest expense of $520 million, which is expected to decrease only slightly over the next 15 years.[10] In other words, the industry has made only a half-penny on every dollar of revenue since deregulation. When this margin of 0.05 percent is compared to other U.S. industries which earned a margin of 5 percent, the benefits of deregulation begin to look like the emperor's new clothes: nonexistent.

Press releases on Delta's earnings over the past several years are symptomatic of this malaise. Delta's PR department consistently highlights revenues but underplays true operating income, expenses and profits. The matter is exacerbated by the fact that much of the non-financial press in some cases incorrectly uses the word "earnings" as a synonym for "revenues." It takes some digging, therefore, to find out that Delta's true net operating income over the past three years is worse than it was four years ago.

Three Ways to Survive Deregulation: Innovation, Intransigence and Cutthroat Competition

In the attempt to understand how deregulation has affected the survival strategies of the airlines, it will prove instructive to examine and appropriate to compare three airlines: American, Delta and Continental. American and Delta are, in brief, members of the "old boy" trunk-carrier club known for their superior service. The Lorenzo-managed Continental, on the other hand, is very like the new kid on the street: hungry, lean and downright mean.

American has managed to protect both its turf and its service reputation and still make money. Much like a gutter fighter whose whole operating premise is to cut an operation to the bone, Continental offers the traveler a low-cost, no-frills, convenient and dependable alternative, hoping to garner a larger market share. By contrast, Delta is that chivalric anomaly, a "gloves-on" competitor. If there was a Marquis of Queensberry rule book for the airline industry competition, Delta would cling to it while the competitors used every trick in the book to win at Delta's expense. Consequently, Delta remains purely reactive to the market forces. Moreover, Delta's operations are bloated by overstaffed departments and, when seeking to enlarge its market shares in places outside of Atlanta, Delta seems unable to either conceive or implement an effective marketing strategy for success. (These points are discussed in greater detail in the chapters that follow.)

AMERICAN AIRLINES: THE INNOVATOR

Although American Airlines opposed deregulation longer than any other major trunk airline, it has adapted best to the new environment by becoming the most innovative airline in the industry. Fortunately for American, both circumstances and its chairman have changed since the days of Albert Casey, who argued for more—rather than less— regulation of the industry.

Since he became chairman of American Airlines, Robert Crandall has provided American with precisely the kind of strong, market-driven leadership required by the deregulation environment. Crandall's credentials as chief executive of an airline are not what one would have expected in the old days, when operations specialists dominated the ranks of the corporate brass. A marketing professional, Crandall has The Right Stuff to lead American Airlines to success in this deregulated marketplace. And in this case the right stuff has meant innovation, innovation, innovation.

Refusing to be shut out of the Southeastern market by Delta and Eastern's strangle hold on Atlanta, American has further expanded its presence in the marketplace by estab- lishing new hubs in the Southeast—Nashville, Tennessee and Raleigh-Durham, North Carolina.

Yet another American Airlines' innovation led the way for U.S. carriers to obtain direct aircraft financing from U.S. manufacturers. This practice was initiated when American arranged with McDonnell-Douglas for a lease-financing agreement that entirely underwrote the acquisition of its MD-80 fleet. Surprisingly, the agreement permits American to walk away from this acquisition program if it chooses to do so. In essence, certain provisions allow for periodic intervals during which American can return the MD-80s to McDonnell-Douglas, paying only modest financial penalties.

Perhaps most importantly, American recognizes that market share depends on networking travel agencies with a highly sophisticated computerized reservations system. It has placed its awesome Sabre computer system into well over 50,000 locations.

Other carriers have followed American's lead in these innovations. Every large trunk carrier in the United States now has a frequent flyer program, with Delta becoming the last major airline to introduce such a program—nearly three years after American.

DELTA: CONSERVATIVE AND SLOW TO CHANGE

Delta is an imitator, preferring to let others take the risks in innovation. Consequently, Delta has followed American's lead, albeit sluggishly, in many of these landmark innovations.

For example, Delta arranged a similar lease-financing agreement with Boeing for the purchase of its B-737 fleet. Delta also introduced the two-tier wage scale for its pilots, but was among the very last to do so and, it now appears, will be the first to eliminate it. In addition, Delta built a hub in Cincinnati and acquired two additional hub operations through its acquisition of Western Air Lines, although it has not introduced any new hubs from a standing start.

Delta's reluctance to innovate may have its most serious consequences in the creation and marketing of a computerized reservations system for travel agencies. Delta delayed three years before introducing a system like American's enormously successful Sabre system. And because Delta has failed to be aggressive in marketing the Datas II system after its introduction, Delta now possesses the lowest market share of any of the five major reservations systems. Because travel agencies write over 90 percent of the airline tickets in this country, such systems as American's Sabre and United's Apollo have emerged as key success factors for the industry.

Also, in sharp contrast to American, since deregulation Delta has not led a *single* major fare innovation that the industry has followed. Shortly after Ron Allen became chairman in 1987, Delta did introduce a discount fare which was higher in price but lower in cancellation fees. It was largely viewed by the industry as an Orwellian effort to impress the public, but it soon disappeared into oblivion.

A prominent business educator told me recently that in his opinion, "The difference that has been so striking is the fact that the two strongest opponents of deregulation, American and Delta, reacted so differently in post-deregulation. Nobody opposed deregulation more intensely than Al Casey at American and Beebe at Delta. But when it became inevitable that deregulation was here to stay, American immediately responded, while Delta floundered."

While they say hindsight is $20/20$, it is interesting to reread the prognosticators of the time to hear how they predicted the outcome of deregulation for Delta. *Fortune* Magazine, for example, noted the obvious in its November 20, 1978 issue with "...the trunks will respond to deregulation in quite different ways because they differ so radically in route structure and in size...." Continuing the common wisdom of the time, *Fortune* predicted that "Fat earnings and a high level of employee productivity make Delta a powerhouse."[11] Predictions were that Delta would concentrate on holding its regular customers with cheaper rates for regular coach and first-class travel and avoid the deep discount fares which were correctly predicted as the natural flow for deregulation.

Unfortunately for Delta, the prediction did not hold. Delta's regular coach and economy fares have been equal to or higher than its competitors, and the much-vaunted high level of employee compensation at Delta, which was supposed to ensure high levels of service and dedication to company goals, has become a wooden saw.

If it did nothing else, deregulation introduced new numbers into the labor-management equation in the airline industry. Under the old system, the CAB calculated fares on a cost-plus basis, thereby giving the airlines no incentive to contain labor expenses. The respective managements of the airlines, through their lawyers, said in effect to the CAB, "Our labor expenses have increased 8 percent in the last three years, and to keep return on equity at the statutory standard, we need another 3 percent fare increase, so we are asking you for an 11 percent fare increase."

The increases in labor costs were usually the result of new union contracts. The bottom line was that the CAB generally granted all, if not a substantial portion, of the requested fare increases. Airline management would simply pass the higher cost of the new contracts, or the new labor cost, to the consumers. Such an environment no longer exists since deregulation, but Delta seems not to have noticed. Witness that when Delta acquired Western in 1986, Delta's average dollar compensation per employee was $51,200; Western's was $36,500.

Rather than cash in on the differential, Delta chose to bring the erstwhile Western employees up to the Delta level immediately. While it would be unrealistic to expect Delta not to bring Western Employees' pay scales up to its own, conventional wisdom suggests that it would have been more effective and certainly more efficient if done through some phase-in process rather than extending the largess of superior Delta benefits from the outset. The majority of formerly Western employees moved from Los Angeles, Western's former headquarters, to Atlanta, a city with a substantially lower cost of living index. Needless to say, those formerly Western employees have made out like veritable bandits.

Labor problems, however, have been a major bane of deregulation and today pose a serious threat to derailing the deregulation experiment. Even though Delta, the highest-cost player in the industry, has escaped major labor problems, distant rumblings are being heard from the employees.

Of the three major opponents of deregulation—Delta, American and Eastern—Delta has done the least to position itself in the deregulated environment. Delta's major strengths at the dawning of deregulation in 1980, were:

- High productivity rate of labor force due to no union constraints;
- Paternalistic company culture offered generous pay raises and a no lay-off policy;
- Owned all of its aircraft, with no leasing;
- Excellent passenger service;
- Remarkably little debt;
- High morale with low turnover, a "highly publicized feeling of family;" and
- Low number of cheap fares.

Of these seven strengths, the only one which has survived deregulation is "excellent passenger service." While true today, the last, "low number of cheap fares," is no longer considered a distinct strength in the new competitive environment. Delta's paternalistic culture is still in place, but it has now become a buzz saw that threatens to chew up the balance sheet as it fosters an attitude of conformity which is not compatible with a need for innovation. Although Delta officials will repeat it incessantly, the argument that the company has a high productivity rate doesn't wash with an analysis of the operating data.

CONTINENTAL: STREET SAVVY

In my opinion, the crucible of the deregulation experiment is Continental Airlines. Once, the formerly Los Angeles-based Continental was the premier small trunk carrier in the southwest and west. Its deluxe cabin service was second to none. But that all changed after Frank Lorenzo and his Texas Air Corporation acquired Continental after a bitter fight in the early '80s. Lorenzo, in order to unshackle Texas Air from the heavy burden of the expenses associated with high wages, particularly that of flight crews at Continental, plunged the airline into Chapter 11 bankruptcy. Reorganized, the company emerged from bankruptcy and today alternates with United as the largest air-carrier system in the free world. Continental pays roughly half of the industry average in compensation and, although it is deplored by its competitors and much of the traveling public, the fact is that through its discount fares which are subject to many restrictions, air travel has become available to a much broader segment of the population of this country.

It has been recently argued by no less a luminary than Tom Peters, co-author of *In Search of Excellence*, that if Lorenzo can introduce the human factor into the equation of his airline management style, then his holding company, which includes both Continental and Eastern, will own the skies of America.

Thanks to Continental, vigorous price wars in air fares are a common event. Continued without abatement, these wars will eventually bring high-cost operators like Delta to their knees.

Some Final Observations on Deregulation

Some of the mixed results of deregulation were not entirely predicted. While it is true that discount fares are, in fact, lower, having risen by less than 75 percent of inflation since 1985, non-discounted air fares have risen 156 percent since 1978 on a constant-dollar basis, a constant that is not adjusted for inflation. Thus, frequent travelers who cannot be flexible in scheduling their air travel must now pay a full fare that is substantially more than they would otherwise pay if fares were still adjusted under the formulae used by the CAB prior to deregulation. Still, air fares in this country are not high enough to permit sustained industry profitability, and it is this latter point which is the most troublesome aspect of deregulation. Service companies that are pressed for dollars become pressed to offer quality service and to perform quality maintenance.

Perhaps the result of deregulation was best summarized by Len Morgan, a retired Braniff captain who writes wistful columns for *Flying* Magazine, in that publication's July 1987 issue:

"For all that may have been wrong with the regulated era, it produced the world's finest airline system. Good service was rendered, passengers paid for what they got and got what they paid for. Fair profits were possible, though by no means assured. Workers enjoyed reasonable security and prospects of comfortable retirement. It was good work with a promising future.

Poor communication is one reason for the present sad state of airline affairs. Had industry and government leaders acted more responsibly in the beginning, we would be enjoying the fruits of sensible reregulation instead of the chaos brought on by cold-turkey deregulation. Had management and labor dealt with each other as teammates instead of as opponents, much of today's infighting would have been avoided. As it is, the industry staggers under billions of dollars of debt, labor-management relations are deteriorating into suspicion and bitterness and no one knows where it is all leading."[12]

At the risk of seeming ambivalent, I can only conclude that deregulation has produced mixed results. The truth is that the balance sheets of this country's airlines have undergone substantial erosion since deregulation. In fact, the debt service of the airline industry is so large today that some analysts predict that in order to avoid "South American loan problems" the creditors of the airlines may soon have to restructure the industry's debt or else the industry will face economic disaster.

From a personal standpoint, deregulation has been a very positive event, as I am the General Counsel of a company that is in the aircraft operating lease business. My company has prospered tremendously since its formation following deregulation because the airlines have awakened to the fact that they are no longer able to own all of their assets and, indeed, must resort to leasing to maintain the fleet diversification that deregulation requires. To that end, I am grateful for deregulation, but at the same time I earnestly believe it has seriously eroded what was the finest air transportation system in the world.

Chapter Two

The Emperor's New Clothes

"There is no such thing as 'soft
sell' or 'hard sell.' There is
only 'smart sell' and 'stupid sell.'"
—Charles Brower

The Invisible Marketing Plan

In the course of writing this book, I had the uncanny feeling
that I was transported into the old folk tale in which the
emperor was duped into thinking that there existed a rare
invisible cloth out of which a suit of clothes had been made
for him. No one would tell him the truth because they had
witnessed the misfortune that seemed to befall messengers
who brought bad news.

For whatever reason, Delta seems to be in that same
predicament. From the press, from the staff, from the PR
Department, all the news is rosy and happy. But the reality
is very different. Nowhere is that more apparent than in
considering Delta's marketing plan or in considering the
absence of Delta's marketing plan.

Marketing Dominates the Airline Business

In mid-1987, Dr. George James, formerly the chief economist
of the Air Transport Association of America and now president of his own firm, Airline Economics, Inc., in Washington, D.C., echoed the sentiment of most industry observers when he said, "One of the most significant lessons to be
learned about U.S. airline deregulation is that marketing has
become supreme in the management structure of the airline.
If the chief executive officer is not already a marketing man,

certainly the marketing voice in that company is among the strongest."[1] In stark contrast to this view is Delta's opinion of itself and its need for strong marketing.

Some eight months after James' remarks were made, I had a brief conversation with Delta's former director of public relations. He bragged that "Delta had no need for a marketing department" because of the strong demand for the carrier's seats out of Atlanta during the summer of 1988. Perhaps this is not so surprising a view for a PR man to espouse, but I have the distinct feeling that this is one case where the PR representative was giving me the management's operational response.

Earlier assessments of Delta have cited its marketing problems. "Delta's biggest challenge is to chart a more aggressive marketing course through the deregulated skies," *Business Week* observed six years ago. A planning chief of one of the major airlines was on record as saying "if there is a deficiency at Delta, it's in marketing. Their response time has been slow."[2] This same view was voiced more recently by Ruben Shohet, a general partner in a venture capital firm and former airline analyst. Shohet expressed to Robert Oppenlander his belief that the Delta marketing department had to be retrenched from top to bottom because it was currently in a hopeless situation.

More recently, in a 1988 speech to those in attendance at an Airline Industry Seminar sponsored by Shearson Lehman Hutton, Dr. James assessed, respectively, the single most critical action each major airline needed to consider in the coming year. Regarding Delta, he said, "Delta needs to continue beefing up its marketing efforts." While more charitable an opinion than Mr. Shohet's, James' comment still reflects a nagging and persistent failure by Delta's management to recognize the central importance of marketing in the deregulated marketplace.

What Delta does not seem to recognize is that deregulation is nothing less than a major paradigm shift, meaning that there has been a significant change in the approach to airline transportation since deregulation including the way we think about airline travel, that is, our conceptual framework for understanding the industry and its dynamics has also changed. Consequently, all the old assumptions must be reevaluated and further assessed. Those which can contribute to success in this new system of functionality may be retained, but most earlier assumptions about the transportation industry no longer hold. Kuhn's dictum that the only way an old paradigm passes from the scene is with the death of the champions of that old set of assumptions,[3] may well identify the reality at Delta. In the airline industry, few management systems can sustain an old paradigm in the face of the market pressures generated by the new operational reality. The remaining question is, will Delta change to embrace the new ideas or will it collapse clinging to its outmoded notions of the place of marketing in the airline industry?

The rest of the industry has long ago recognized the importance of marketing and strategic marketing management in the airline industry, yet there is no discernible change at Delta. Marketing has become critical because it is the means by which carriers can differentiate themselves to their agents and their buying public. The airline business has virtually become a commodity business. Prior to deregulation, airlines had no reason to be concerned with differentiation. The Civil Aeronautics Board performed that function for carriers, distinguishing them by region and city, and determining rate structure for the industry as a whole. Under those circumstances, marketing's function was to promote air travel within the cities that the airlines served and to support or oversee the marketing representatives in servicing travel agencies and corporate accounts.

Two developments in the wake of deregulation changed the role of marketing in the airline industry: competition and computerization of passenger service and travel agencies. Delta appears to have failed to assess accurately the significance of these developments and, in so doing, has missed some important opportunities to strengthen its competitive position in the industry. This is particularly unfortunate, given Delta's happy distinction of having the industry's strongest balance sheet. Had Delta taken the offensive when such rivals as United were in weakened positions, it could have secured a stronger long-term position for itself. Now, it faces increased competition from United, with Stephen Wolf at the helm there, along with American Airlines, widely regarded of late as the industry's best-managed and most innovative carrier.

Underestimating the Competition

Delta's problem in the marketing arena has to do with its definition of what constitutes marketing, its complete lack of strategic planning, and its total fixation upon one competitor—Eastern. Delta has neglected the strategic aspects of the business in favor of tactics, most of which are knee-jerk reactions to Eastern Airlines, its presumed arch rival. In 1982, Joseph A. Cooper, then Delta's senior vice president for marketing, explained Delta's sluggishness in moving toward computerization this way: "Had Eastern been full speed ahead" [in computerizing passenger service and travel agencies in the 1970s, rather than American and United], "we would have been more active."[4]

It is incredible that the senior marketing officer would openly admit that his company was charting its marketing course exclusively as a reaction to strategies by Eastern Airlines, a company that Delta's management loves to ridicule. But this is precisely what Cooper stated that Delta was doing. Cooper was not long for the job, but the corporate view seems not to have changed substantially since he left.

Although Delta has had a halcyon year in 1988, the quality of its earnings seem suspect. Nevertheless, demand for airline seats is strong, and the economy continues to perk along. More important for Delta is the contraction of Eastern in Atlanta, which has given Delta the opportunity, though one perhaps short-lived, to virtually *own* Atlanta.

In the summer of 1988, Delta has literally been feeding on the carrion of a decaying Eastern, which The Wall Street Journal described charitably as the "incredible shrinking airline."[5] It is estimated that through its contraction,

Eastern has lost 15 to 20 percent of its market share in Atlanta in 1988. In fact, in June 1988, Eastern reduced the number of its Atlanta-based flights from approximately 350 to 280 per day, the lowest for Eastern since 1974, six years before the current Hartsfield Atlanta International Airport was opened.

Such an increase in market share does not represent hard-won concessions from a strong competitor, however. Instead, it owes its existence more to a structural monopoly than to any real competitive triumph. That slack is being taken up mostly by Delta only because of the hammerlock on gate facilities in Atlanta it shares with Eastern.

This fortuity may not continue, and yet the marketing department at Delta is even more complacent than ever. If Lorenzo disposes of Eastern, as he probably should do, he will no doubt replace it in Atlanta with low-cost Continental. Eastern's unions are claiming that Texas Air is deliberately shrinking their unionized carrier and transferring routes and assets to Continental. As an alternative, Lorenzo might reconstitute Eastern in the manner of Continental, and return it to Atlanta as a low-cost operator to compete head-on with Delta. If either case occurs, given Delta's high operating costs, Delta's halcyon days will be gone unless it reacts by becoming a more aggressive marketing company.

Delta has not been so quick to respond to its other far more viable competitors. It seems not to have noticed that in 1982 American Airlines announced its future marketing strategy for toe-to-toe competition in roughly three-quarters of Delta's markets. Since that announcement, American has established a new hub with brand-new airport facilities in Nashville and the same in Raleigh-Durham. In anticipation of the near-term woes of Hartsfield Airport, American has adopted a "flank the enemy" approach to Atlanta and is providing alternatives for passengers connecting in the Southeast to by-pass Atlanta by using the Nashville and Raleigh-Durham hubs. Indeed, American advertises itself in the Southeast as the "attractive alternative." This appeals to those passengers who wish to avoid both the inconvenience of a connection in Atlanta, where Hartsfield's immense physical plant often means walking great distances on concourses, and the higher fares charged by Eastern and Delta out of Atlanta.

After a relatively short period of time operating its substantially expanded Raleigh-Durham and Nashville hubs, American has become Eastern's second-largest competitor, after Delta, in those cities. If there is an Eastern strike, American should enjoy an additional windfall as travelers seek alternatives to booked-up Delta flights through Atlanta.

How does Delta, the competitor, fare in the lair of the American tiger? The short answer is, not very well. But what can be expected when Delta seems not even to notice the tiger exists, let alone that it is being stalked.

According to published sources, Dallas was Delta's biggest post-deregulation priority. With its usual hoopla, Delta announced in 1980 that it planned to build a Dallas hub half the size of Atlanta's, and at that time Delta/Atlanta serviced 315 flights per day.[6] In the competition for major markets out of Dallas, Delta has managed to capture less than half of American's market share, even though in most cases American manages to derive more revenue per passenger mile from its market share.

"American has simply clobbered Delta in Dallas," one analyst observed. "In addition to outcarrying Delta in Texas, American has driven its rival out of the important Dallas/LaGuardia market, the routing most Dallas business travelers to New York prefer."[7]

Indeed, after nearly ten years of trying, Delta now holds approximately 23 percent of the Dallas-Ft. Worth market, but most of that has come out of the hides of other weakened competitors, like Braniff. American retains a seemingly impregnable 60 percent share in its home base. Even substantially expanded operations in Dallas created by Delta's acquisition of Western have failed to nudge American's market share. In the face of American's marketing prowess, Delta's competitive impotence is just another index of how wrong Delta is to devalue the importance of marketing.

For example, in the Dallas/New York market, which is Delta's sixth largest market system-wide, American had a 45.3 percent market share versus Delta's 18.3 percent share in the third quarter of 1986.[8] Even more compelling is that with its 45.3 percent market share, American's yield was 11.04 cents per revenue passenger mile compared with Delta's yield of 8.64. Stated another way, this yield difference suggests that, by a ratio of almost three to one, passengers traveling round-trip from Dallas to New York would rather pay roughly 1.5 cents per mile more to fly American! So where is the much-vaunted Delta quality of service differential?

In Los Angeles, another major market from Dallas, American has a 40 percent market share versus 23 percent for Delta, and American earns a revenue yield of 13.7 cents versus Delta's 12.2 cents.

Similarly, in the Dallas/San Francisco market, American has a market share of 40.4 percent with a yield of 10.09 cents versus Delta's market share of 24.8 percent with a 9.27-cent yield.

This competitive situation in Dallas points up a classic example of effective marketing. Two airlines, each rated superior for their service, compete head on. Delta obtains its market share at the cost of the other weaker carriers in the market. American captures the lead and maintains its market share with its well-orchestrated, innovative marketing management.

While American's lopsided victory in Dallas is no doubt skewed by the strong bias there for its Sabre computerized reservations system, which demonstrates how a strong computer system can provide a formidable competitive advantage, the clear preference for American in Dallas also may be attributed to the "home town" influence. Some travel agency comments received during a survey (see Chapter 3) indicate that there is a partial bias in the larger cities for airlines headquartered therein. For example, there seems to be a heavy favoritism towards United in the Chicago markets, but then again that could be a function of United's superb computer reservations system, Apollo.

In Atlanta, there is more of an anomaly. Delta has long been considered the premier carrier in the Southeast and, certainly, in Atlanta. In the Atlanta/Dallas market, Delta is the predominant carrier, and American has only a minuscule share. This, however, has nothing to do with marketing or quality of service; given the tight control Delta and Eastern wield over the gates at Hartsfield Airport, American has virtually no opportunity to come into Atlanta with any great strength, even if it wanted to.

Lack of gate opportunities has also prevented United Air Lines from penetrating the Southeastern market. United's Stephen Wolf salivates at the thought of getting the opportunity to compete head-on with Delta in Atlanta. As one observer has mentioned, Delta has always kept a low profile, has never spent heavily for frills and has always been the preferred trunk airline for passengers from the Southeast. "That semi-ethnic base carried them for years," said the president of another big airline. "But as their relatively less aggressive marketing policies get out of Atlanta, they are less effective...."9

Delta certainly does not enjoy the home-town advantages, as do American and United, of excellent computerized reservations systems. From the travel agency perspective at least, this means Delta is not faring as well at home. Despite the fact that most of the travel agencies in Atlanta interviewed for this book gratuitously volunteered the view that Delta is a good company to work with, many still don't use Delta's reservations system.

The mounting importance of travel agencies in the sale of airline seats and the value of computerized reservations systems as the key to influencing agencies' airline recommendations leaves Delta dangerously exposed to competitive challenges even on its home turf. A dramatic example of that is evidenced by the fact that in Atlanta, Delta's

Datas II is used by only 21.6 percent of the travel agencies in the city. In contrast, 24.1 percent use American's Sabre and 27.2 percent use United's Apollo system. Even more dramatic is the fact that in Dallas, 85 percent of the travel agencies use American's Sabre system and only 4.1 use Delta's Datas II.[10]

Delta's Self-Satisfaction

In 1985, some five years after Delta opened its Dallas hub, an interesting interview was conducted by and published in *Travel Weekly*, the widely respected newspaper for the travel industry. In the context of that interview, comments by Whitley Hawkins, then the new senior vice president marketing for Delta, reveal Delta's complacency toward its position in the industry.

> TW: "I'd like to ask you something generically.... Many people feel that there will be only four or five big airlines in a few years. Obviously, United is going to be one of them, especially if the Pan Am deal goes through.
> Bob Crandall and a few other people in Dallas would like American to be. You have a reputation for not being that aggressive, actually, in the outside world. Do you think you are going to be one of those four or five?"
> Hawkins: "Sure."
> TW: "How can you do that if you don't merge with somebody or become more aggressive?"
> Hawkins: "I think if you ask our competitors you will find we are more aggressive than most people give us credit for being. We are just *quietly aggressive*."[11]

One prominent airline analyst disagrees, claiming Delta has sound management, but they've never had to scrap because they have competed against Eastern and been in Atlanta all their lives. The question is whether it knows how to be aggressive. If it knows how to be aggressive, Delta has failed to demonstrate it.

The Failure to Innovate

Delta Air Lines does not innovate if it has a choice. The corporate culture at Delta does not honor innovation; it honors loyalty to tradition. Innovation requires acceptance of change, and Delta has fostered an arrogance among its members that believes nothing is better than Delta or Delta's ways. This attitude suggests a cult mentality that is self-centered, self-serving and potentially self-destructive. Most of all, it is truly regrettable.

I remember that I shared that arrogance during my years at Delta. I can recall sitting across the table from lawyers with other airlines and actually feeling sorry for them because they worked for companies other than Delta!

Delta heightens its arrogance by insulating itself from the larger airline community. As a rule, it does not participate in industry concerns. Recently, Delta declined to attend an industry-wide conference, claiming there would be too much proprietary information discussed which would disadvantage Delta. In truth, Delta has lagged behind other carriers in the subject matter which was the focus of the conference and could have benefited most by participating in an industry conference on that subject.

Delta's approach to innovations is reactive, not proactive. When innovations are introduced into the industry and when Delta perceives a threat to its turf, it will grudgingly react. However in these cases, Delta seems to match the competition by structuring its own incentive programs with built-in disincentives. For example, three years after other airlines had led the way, Delta finally introduced its own computerized reservations system. Despite its desperate need to play an aggressive game of catch-up, Delta refused to build into its sales package any mechanism designed to help customers in buying out their existing contracts with other computer reservations systems. That the competition considers such buy-out assistance a very important part of their efforts to place their systems in the offices of travel agents seems to have escaped Delta. Only recently, five years after Datas II was introduced, has Delta offered modest buy-out incentives, and so remains far behind other carriers in its efforts to sell Datas II.

When Delta does make some effort to create a marketing strategy, it is frequently ill-thought-out. Given that in the airline industry travel agents are responsible for the vast majority of reservations, it would be in Delta's best interest to keep the travel agents happy. So what did Delta do? Late in 1984, Delta cranked up its hoopla machine and right there in front of the entire industry announced that Delta had reached a special agreement with General Electric to offer substantial discounts for its traveling executives in return for a commitment of volume. This announcement meant, of course, that rather than nurturing its relationship with the nation's travel agencies, Delta was going head-to-head in competition with them. As a consequence, thousands of these agencies would lose the G.E. business because the company was dealing directly with the supplier of its air services. Some travel agencies have never forgiven Delta. None was forewarned, and Delta seemed not to know that it had made a major tactical mistake.

Delta's competitors did not follow suit. For good reason! Many were pointedly disdainful of Delta's move. "There's no such animal as volume discounts for individual corporations" at United, noted John Zeeman, UAL's executive vice president of marketing and planning. Direct corporate discounting is not attractive, Zeeman continued, because it "... does not generate any new business. All that will happen is that the corporation will be able to take more trips for the same amount of money, and the airlines will lose."[12]

Another example of a grudging reaction to a threat from competitive innovation may be found in Delta's attempt to be creative with its fares. A little more than three weeks after he became chairman, the press began heralding Ron Allen as Delta's marketing savior. Beneath a photo of Allen featured in *The Atlanta Constitution's* business section, a caption bugled, "Chairman Ronald Allen is believed planning to market Delta more aggressively."[13] The accompanying story was headlined "Delta to Restructure Its Discount Rates." The Delta marketing cognoscenti had created a new discount fare for Delta that was, in fact, *higher* than prevailing rates, but in essence gave the passenger half of the fare back if he or she canceled. The pitch was that there was no refund under the traditional deep-discount fares, so here was Delta providing one. *Voila!*

Within three days, the Aviation Consumer Action Project, along with Public Citizen, a non-profit group in Washington, D.C., lashed out at the Delta fares and put Delta immediately on the defensive. "I don't see how raising ticket prices helps consumers," said Cornish Hitchcock, an attorney with Public Citizen, explaining that under Delta's plan the lowest fares would be raised to compensate for reducing the cancellation penalty from 100 percent to only 50 percent, a plan he alleged was totally unfair.

Side-stepping the simple arithmetic of the matter by invoking obtuse logic, Delta's spokesman Bill Berry countered, "No way are we looking at this as a fare hike ... You can't make a comparison, because these fares are totally different. It is like comparing apples and oranges."[14] An Atlanta reporter thought "lemons" was perhaps more appropriate. In any case, the fare proposal soon faded into oblivion.

Delta has contributed few fare introductions, most of which have not been matched by other carriers or sustained for any period of time.[15] In the complex arena of airline fares, American and Texas Air stand out as the leading fare innovators in this country; the other carriers lag behind in some degree or another. Delta remains the least innovative player in this strategic marketplace, as it has introduced only one fare that was sustained or followed by the other carriers.

As the history of fare introductions illustrates, Delta is at the mercy of its competition in yet another important way. If the company is unable to originate, implement and sustain those fares which will allow it to be competitive and yet maintain some profit, it must suffer a fate dictated by its competitors.

When the marketing gurus at Delta did come up with a truly original contribution to the world of the frequent flyer, it soon became controversial and, some say, disastrous to the industry. In late 1987, Delta announced a triple mileage bonus program for frequent flyers which would go into effect in January 1988. The only restriction was that tickets had to be purchased using the American Express Card. That other major carriers were forced to match the program drew criticism from industry spokesmen:

— "It's a foolish program, a mistake that will lose money for the industry," said Bob Crandall, American's chairman.[16]

— "A monumental mistake," said David Sylvester, an airline analyst at Kidder, Peabody & Co., Inc.[17]

— "...just plain dumb," said John Zeeman, the executive vice president for marketing and planning at United Air Lines.[18]

— "Only a fool would tell you that this is not fraught with problems for the industry and for frequent fliers," said James O'Donnell, Continental Air Lines' vice president of marketing services.[19]

Responded Delta's public relations spokesman Jim Lundy: "We don't see it as a form of price competition, we see it as a marketing man's tool ... This was an excellently researched programme which was designed very carefully with American Express."[20]

Needless to say, Delta's one innovation is still causing a furor throughout the industry.

One immediate reaction came from the Internal Revenue Service, which has long looked askance at "freebies" that relate to transportation. The Internal Revenue Service began deliberations to determine whether triple bonus mileage awards should be reported by recipients as ordinary income and taxed accordingly. The IRS has since put the subject on hold, but the magnitude of the increase in bonus miles makes the free travel issue more compelling to the IRS, which believes that free travel should be taxed as income.

Perhaps a more spectacular result of the triple mileage program has been the creation of a task force of the American Institute of Certified Public Accountants to develop new rules designed to force airlines to face the new realities on their balance sheet. The final rules, which would have to be approved by the Financial Accounting Standards Board, could take effect as early as the end of 1988 or early 1989. Julius Maldutis of Salomon Brothers notes that one proposal would require airlines to record the equivalent of 10 percent of their passenger revenue as a liability, indicating a potential industry-wide revenue loss of $3.5 billion in the 1988 triple mileage aspect of the program alone.

The effect of the accounting changes is the subject of considerable debate. "You can no longer say that the revenue process is substantially complete when the ticket is sold," argues Thomas Sinton, head of the AICPA task force that drafted the rules. "Passengers are purchasing tickets with the expectation of a free flight, and we have to account for that liability."[21]

Under the task force's proposed guidelines, each air carrier would be required to hold out a portion of revenue from each ticket and create a "liability reserve account." The most ambitious proposal, however, would require the carriers to make a cumulative catch-up adjustment to account for their current liabilities through the end of their current fiscal year. That would mean a big one-time hit to income. Think of it as an airline's version of a bank's loan-loss reserves for Latin lending—although the airline's reserve will eventually be taken into income.

While it was hailed early on by Wall Street as a "sound and conservative Delta-like program" because it was tied to purchases of tickets only through the American Express card, someone at Delta should have anticipated the reaction of the other airlines. Their reaction: triple mileage bonuses with no strings attached; buy the ticket and you get triple mileage.

To be fair, Delta's decision to initiate the triple mileage bonus program was, from its own perspective, at least, a wise thing to do. The company has the lowest load factor in the U.S. airline industry, which means that at any given time it is flying around the country with more seats available per airplane than any other U.S. carrier. Thus, Delta felt that it had little to lose by implementing the triple mileage program. Even so, if the accounting proposals are adopted, it portends a weakening of Delta's balance sheet. The program will probably have more adverse effect on other members of the industry—except American—than on Delta. It is hard to believe, however, that Delta could not have foreseen the consequences of the other airlines' reactions. They immediately countered with expanded versions of the triple mileage program which required no particular finance company to write the tickets to obtain the triple mileage awards. That Delta seems not to have anticipated such reaction is additional evidence of its insular thinking.

Some industry analysts have recently begun to see the whole concept of the program as a self-inflicted wound. Kidder, Peabody & Co., Inc. analyst, David Sylvester, estimated that the promotion would reduce industry profits by $150 million in 1989. Another analyst predicted that by the end of 1988 the airlines would face a potential revenue loss of $1.24 billion from frequent flyer programs. Delta itself stands to lose up to $140 million in revenue loss as a result of spawning this tragic program.[22]

The industry's worst nightmare — free flyers cashing in over a short period of time and gobbling up revenue-producing seats on many flights—might be imminent. In 1984, when Pan American World Airways initiated a program designed to force frequent flyers to use their awards or lose them, the resulting chaos triggered a $50 million revenue loss for Pan Am. On one memorable occasion during this chaos, the nightmare became reality. A Pan American B-747 was filled to capacity and ready to depart from JFK to London. When the company checked the manifest it realized that every seat on the aircraft was filled by a frequent flyer trying to travel before the program expired!

Analyst Julius Maldutis of Salomon Brothers has expressed concern about the triple mileage program. "The industry is facing a far greater menace [from the triple mileage program] than in any price wars of the past," said

Maldutis. He estimated potential revenue loss by the end of 1988 at $1.24 billion, with $940 million due to triple mileage awards alone. The results of triple mileage promotions is that financial short-term gains are purchased at an unknown expense in future periods.[23]

There have already been casualties of this industry madness. Midway Airlines in Chicago suffered a $5,360,000 net loss for the first quarter of 1988, a $6.4 million swing from a $1.1 million net profit in the same period in 1987. Midway's operating loss was $2.2 million against an operating income of $1.6 million in the same period in 1987. Chairman and CEO David R. Hinson said that the first quarter results are almost totally the result of "... soft traffic in January and February resulting from the 'Triple Mileage' programs instituted by Midway's competitors."[24]

How did Delta react to its competitors' expansion of triple mileage programs which do not stipulate how tickets are bought? Tearing a page from its own slim volume on competitive practices in such matters, Delta's senior marketing vice president Whitley Hawkins called the competition's response "a knee jerk competitive reaction."[25] Did he really expect the competition to sit still while Delta stole the march? Given this program and the treacherous potential which it imposes, the industry might be money ahead to pay Delta not to innovate.

Misguided Sales Force

That the Delta sales force seems unable to be aggressive in selling its system may reflect more of who they are than what they know. Delta's national sales force, called "field marketing representatives," are responsible for selling and providing service to travel agents and corporate accounts. Representatives' reports go to a district director who is responsible for all regional sales activity including the activities of reservation agents in regional offices. The district directors report to an assistant VP in Atlanta so that all marketing policy and planning is centralized in Atlanta.

Discussions with travel agents suggest that marketing is too centralized and field representatives are kept on a very short string. That is to say, they are not given sufficient latitude to make on-the-spot decisions on a range of marketing policies without conferring with someone in Atlanta. Almost as if by design, these constraints limit their advantage in competitive situations. For example, although it is standard practice among Delta's competitors to sell their reservations systems by offering to assist travel agencies in buy-outs of other carriers' systems, it is only very recently that Delta authorized its marketing representatives to negotiate such buy-outs—but only on a very selective basis. Generally, however, in apparent complete disregard of its position at a very distant last place in the computerized reservations systems race, Delta has maintained a steadfast policy of not helping its potential clients buy out competitor's leases on their systems. Delta seems almost haughty in this regard, as if to say, "We have a superior product, and if you don't recognize that fact, it's too bad for you!"

Marketing representative positions are considered choice spots at Delta, and are much sought after. These are not entry-level positions; representatives are drawn from the ranks of Delta insiders—marketing and finance staffers as well as flight attendants. An important criterion which governs the selection of these candidates is how well they can represent Delta and project the Delta image. A forceful personality and good looks are highly regarded traits in such selection processes.

For many people, the sales force—in addition to flight attendants and reservation agents—is the embodiment of Delta, and as such these individuals create a most positive impression. Time and again, in my discussions with travel agents and frequent flyers, I would hear about the people at Delta. One of the pluses travel agents often reported was that passengers describing their experience with Delta to their respective agencies consistently mentioned the good service they were given by those Delta people who had interacted directly with them. Delta is correct when it says its people are its greatest asset.

Unfortunately, once they have selected an attractive sales force, Delta refuses to give it the authority to be as effective as it could be. This is due in large part to a striking lack of leadership in Atlanta. Moreover, although the Delta sales force is staffed with attractive personalities, it comes up short when judged on the basis of technical skill, customer support and accommodation, local authority to offer incentives to match customer needs and expectations, and a clear sense of purpose or direction. These are characteristics that provide competitive advantage and they are usually the result of training programs designed by an effective marketing department.

According to a senior program analyst at Delta, field representatives are neither technically sophisticated nor trained to use computer reservations systems. She believes Delta's latest version of its reservations system, called DeltaStar, is vastly superior to the earlier version of Datas II. She proposed to an assistant VP of marketing, who supported her proposal, that she receive training in the advantages of DeltaStar over its competitors and be permitted to sell the system to agents and serve as a technical product manager for field staff. Senior marketing executives rebuffed the proposal on the grounds that it was impractical to have its field representatives so specialized in one particular area and that the marketing representatives had to continue to be "generalists."

Nowhere are these competitive characteristics more critical than in the arena of travel agencies and in the selling of computer reservations systems. True to form, Delta's leadership still continues to procrastinate in the creation of an adequate training program designed to prepare the sales force to compete effectively.

While it is standard practice in most sales forces that the sales representatives are the front lines of any attempt at competitive analysis, Delta seems to believe that it does not need to use its sales force to gather insights about Delta's customers. At one time, the company would contact senior executives, particularly those who were in what is that now elite group called "The Flying Colonels," and ask their opinions on Delta's service. Even that minimal competitive intelligence-gathering process is no longer a part of the Delta marketing scheme. In short, the company seems to have lost touch with both the current status of the competition and the satisfaction of its clients.

What will it take to get the leadership to recognize that they should give the highest priority to locking in the business of travel agencies by the installation of Delta's reservations system? Where are the potent incentives the sales team can bring to bear secure this goal? Delta seems determined not to provide its sales force with either the necessary competitive analyses of other systems or the program of regular training required to increase their technical skills and to enable them to demonstrate enhancements when added to the system. Such lack of support for the sales staff is clear evidence that Delta continues to believe that attractive personalities alone can turn the tide in a high-tech industry. In another era, perhaps, this would have been true. In the deregulated, market-driven and computer-intensive airline industry at the end of the 1980s that will never be true.

Failure of the Atlanta Marketing Management Team

Strategic marketing has never been permitted a strong voice at Delta. For all intents and purposes, marketing continues to function as if it were a pre-deregulation sales and advertising department. The only innovations have been the addition of two departments devoted to the computer reservations system and yield management. Within marketing, even these new departments were initiated grudgingly long after it became apparent that these were important elements of the competition's success in mounting effective intrusions into Delta's traditional territory.

The failure of the highly centralized Delta marketing team lies in the quality of the personnel who run it. During the tumultuous years since deregulation, Delta has had only two senior marketing executives. The first, Joseph Cooper, was in place at the time deregulation was enacted. He was a protege of Thomas M. Miller, his predecessor, who had promoted such fares as the "Owly Bird and Early Bird" and believed that the best and only advertisement that Delta, or any other airline, needed was to reproduce the schedules in local newspapers. Cooper attempted to maintain Miller's strategy at Delta and hence was completely caught off guard when deregulation brought changes into the industry. After a tumultuous time in the early 1980s, Cooper elected to take early retirement.

Second in line for this marketing post was Whitley Hawkins, another Delta "lifer" who has spent his entire career at Delta and who was promoted to the senior marketing post upon Cooper's retirement. Hawkins had been a sales representative for Delta and then assistant vice president of marketing prior to being named senior vice president of marketing. Knowledgable insiders say that Hawkins is Ron Allen's "yes man" when it comes to marketing issues, and that he came to the post over the head of R. A. McKinnon, who had been his boss. Tony McKinnon was a straight shooter, and Allen did not like his candor. At the time of Hawkins' promotion, Allen was chief operating officer and the senior vice president of marketing reported to him. The marketing group still reports to Allen in his new position as CEO.

The current COO, Hollis Harris, has a background in operations, which covers flight attendants, pilots and properties. Another Georgia Tech graduate and Delta lifer, Harris has no background in marketing.

Neither is, for that matter, Ron Allen a marketing expert. Like his predecessor, Dave Garrett, Ron Allen is an engineer by training, and his functional experience prior to upper-level management was in personnel. In general, it is fair to say that while engineers are taught principles and facts, they are not trained to think either creatively or intuitively. Engineers are trained to be attentive to details, and usually find it difficult to take in what gifted marketing people more easily conceptualize as "the big picture." To leave strategic marketing in the hands of "yes men" and engineers is to leave it in the least capable hands.

The result of such failure to engage the most talented marketing skills available has been to leave Delta vulnerable to the marketing prowess of those who know its value. However, given Delta's penchant for promoting from within, it is not likely this failure in Atlanta is going to change any time soon.

But what explains this policy for the continuity of failure? Unhappily for Delta, there seems to be a flawed philosophy at work here. It is a philosophy endemic to many institutions where sinecures are coveted too highly. In such institutions, it seems, the mediocre will always prefer to promote others who are equally mediocre. If individuals who are gifted and skilled are nowhere to be seen on the corporate playing field, then mediocrity does not suffer by comparison and may appear to be excellence personified. That is a grim hypothesis.

The Marketing Budget

Delta's shortcomings in marketing raise not only a people question, but also one of money. Since 1978, in the fiercely growing competitive airline environment, Delta has remained significantly below average airline industry advertising and publicity costs as expressed in terms of numbers of passengers flown. In 1986, for example, Delta spent $1.85 per passenger while the average for the industry was $2.83. On the high side, United spent $4.31 and TWA $4.49.

If reservations and sales expenses are added to advertising and publicity expenses, Delta exceeds the industry average every year, with the exception of 1981, since 1978. This further points out Delta's emphasis on personal contact through its reservations and sales people. While this is commendable and has indeed assisted Delta in maintaining its profitability in the past, given the deficiencies in its computerized reservations system and the failure to provide technical training for the sales force, personal contacts may begin to mean less and less to the users, principally the travel agents. Certainly, personal contacts alone will not carry the day in the current environment.

Delta: Living in the Past

In fiscal 1983, when Delta reported a $16.1 million loss, it attributed its problems to misjudging the economy. Tony

McKinnon, then VP for marketing, said Delta had expected a recovery and had held discount seats too long, too tight and, as a result, had lost traffic. Robert Oppenlander, then senior VP for finance as well as CFO, responded to the charge that Delta had failed to adjust its long-held policies to changing market conditions, claiming, "We're responding to the intensity of the [price] competition, but I don't think you can say we are changing our nature."[26] Oppenlander was correct six years ago, and that statement is echoed by Delta today.

On adapting to change, Dr. George James, the president of Airline Economics, Inc., recently remarked that attempts to hold on to ways of the past have led to financial losses or management replacement in the airlines industry. "Every management in the new environment has had to make changes and has had to learn to take risks. Still, several have not moved fully up to the front in this regard," James said.

Delta's management prefers to live in the past and the simple facts are these: First, Delta seems to loathe innovation perhaps because innovation represents coming to grips with the future. Innovation, when it comes, is permitted grudgingly and, when permitted, is nearly always undercut in some way which weakens it substantially.

Second, Delta clings to the past by covering itself in the bogus laurels of a "people-to-people" company. This is all very well and good, but such a strategy cannot substitute for either good training and technical expertise of its sales force or in the constantly increasing need for superior hardware/software interface that is vital to this computer-intensive industry.

Third, as a marketing team, the senior management at Delta remains backward. The failure to take advantage of opportunities and simple state-of-the-art marketing practices is evidence of ineptitude.

How long this great company will labor under such handicaps and yet sustain its market share, I do not know.

Chapter Three

This Little Airline Went to Market; This Little Airline Stayed Home

"If we are to recover prosperity
we shall have to find ways of
emancipating energy and enterprise
from the frustrating control
of timid ignoramuses."
—Prince Philip,
Duke of Edinburgh

Marketing Delta

"Anyone who doesn't work for Delta is in that great holding pattern in the sky," Tom Beebe bragged at the annual service awards dinner in the Spring of 1978. Tony McKinnon, then assistant vice president of marketing for Delta and until recently vice president marketing for American Airlines, nearly gagged on his rubber chicken, and I distinctly remember biting my tongue. "Buster Tom," as he was unaffectionately known, had just made another profoundly absurd pronouncement, an ability for which he was justly famous.

If there is any company in the industry which is "in that great holding pattern in the sky," especially when it comes to working with the all-important travel agency side of the industry, it is Delta. Travel agents in the United States handle over 90 percent of airline ticket sales in all categories, including discount travel, pleasure travel, business travel and international travel.

Computerized Reservations Systems

Since the advent of the computer transformed airline reservations systems into the lifeblood of the airline industry,

there has never been a more potent opportunity to expand
sales or promote a company's service than is now presented
by company-owned computerized reservations systems
which can link up with a computer terminal in each travel
agency in the nation.

In fact, some of the more visionary airline analysts
predict that in the not-too-distant future an airline company
will own only a computerized reservations system and,
given the attractive financial returns of such an arrangement, lease everything else. In recent years, for example,
American Airlines has consistently realized an average
return on investment on the order of 20 percent from its
superlative Sabre computer reservations system. One airline
analyst has suggested that if American were to concentrate
its efforts on Sabre and shed its less profitable airline business, it would make more money in its first year of operations than Delta does as an airline.

What are computerized reservations systems and
why have they emerged as such an important internal force?
Essentially, they are proprietary software programs owned
by the airlines, which lease them to travel agencies and to
large travel departments of corporations. The software programs will execute the basic booking of the airline ticket and
seat selection. The more sophisticated programs will make
hotel and rental car reservations and even set up tours for
business conventions. The more sophisticated one carrier's
software program is, the more likely travel agencies are to
lease that system. That the airline owner is both the landlord
of the system and the fixer of the problems that might
develop within the system establishes an immediate presence within the travel agency. The concomitant result is that
the carrier which owns the system is likely to get more
business from that travel agency; a carrier whose system is
not leased by the agency gets less business. Since travel
agents write such a significant percentage of airline tickets
in this country, it stands to reason that the carrier with the
best and most widely used system has a distinctive advantage for increasing its market share.

The Competition

It is safe to say that American's Sabre system is Delta's chief competitive advantage. As the reality of deregulation was setting in, in early 1980, American purchased a basic computerized reservations system—Sabre. Today, just eight years later, Sabre is the single most important internal force in the airline industry in terms of sales of tickets worldwide. The combination of Sabre's capacity and substantial time advantage in its existing base of installations at travel agencies creates a competitive disadvantage for Delta that Delta may never overcome. Indeed, the current management does not seem interested in overcoming that disadvantage.

Other airlines followed American's lead. The Apollo system, purchased by United shortly after American's purchase of Sabre, is only marginally behind Sabre in terms of its speed and flexibility. Eastern, which purchased System One now owned by Texas Air, gets high marks in versatility.

Datas II

For three long years after the purchase of Sabre, while American stole the march on Delta, Delta remained without a computerized reservations system. In 1983 Delta announced that it had purchased, at an awesome cost of $130 million, a reservation system called Datas II.

When Delta made its announcement of the new system, the single and only prominent marketing feature in Delta's announcement was that it had "no seat selection bias and therefore its versatility virtually outmoded all of the other reservations systems then in current use." The first part of the statement was true enough at the time. However, it was well known to Delta and to the entire airline industry that the U.S. Justice Department had launched an investigation into the bias inherent in American's and United's computerized reservations systems. Instead this bias favored seat selection on their flights when travel agents used either airline's computer reservations systems, and seat selection bias constituted a possible violation of the antitrust laws since American and United systems combined accounted for more than 70 percent of the airline ticket sales in the United States.

When Joseph Cooper, Delta's senior vice president of marketing, made the statement that Datas II had no seat bias, he meant that the system listed flights in a strictly chronological order, without regard to airline selection. At the time, both Apollo and Sabre would favor flights for American and United respectively. According to allegations of competitors of United and American as well as the Justice Department, competing airlines were difficult to reach through the system inasmuch as the program made it difficult when it was required to call up information regarding the flight of another airline.

A mere six months after Delta had purchased its expensive Datas II, the Justice Department settled the "seat bias" issue with American and United on a consent decree basis. From that time on, the issue of seat selection bias had lost its force in the marketplace. If you call a travel agent who uses the Sabre system, the chances are good the agent will put you on American, if it is a possibility. Like many of its public pronouncements, Delta's statement that Datas II had outmoded all other systems is as inaccurate today as it was in 1983.

Why Did Delta Delay?

The salient questions here are why Delta waited so long to enter the market with a computerized reservations system and why, when it did finally introduce a system, was that system so strategically inferior? The answer to both questions is that Delta's marketing force was in turmoil. For example, Bill Atchinson, vice president of computer services and computer department head, was forced into early retirement. Similarly, Joseph Cooper, senior vice president of marketing, took early retirement because of the total disarray in Delta's marketing department. Confusion was not a small element at play in Delta's troubles.

Why the disarray? Observers close to the scene say that there was an all-out internecine war at Delta between those in marketing who desperately wanted to upgrade Delta's aging computerized reservations system and the computer services staff. Long after the industry had gone to the automatic printout of boarding passes, at Delta the boarding pass still had to be manually prepared. In fact, a number of Delta employees claim it was the parsimonious Robert Oppenlander, senior vice president of finance, who led the opposition to modernization. Never known for its industry participation, Delta's executives did not confer with their peers in the industry to determine what, in fact, was the state of the art in airline computerized reservations systems, a failing for which Delta pays a price daily.

James Martin, a consultant and author based in Bermuda, observed several airlines suffered setbacks because they took too long developing reservations systems for travel agents. As a result, Martin says, travel agents gave most of their business to American and United because those carriers first produced the systems that saved them time and money by letting them make reservations through central computer operations. American, in fact, now makes more money from its travel service's computer booking operation than from its airline business. Also, United and American benefited because, at least initially, their systems gave preferential treatments to their own flights.[1]

From the Horse's Mouth

I had a discussion with the principal of a travel agency in Atlanta during the course of the research for this book, and I asked her, simply, "What is your opinion of Delta?" After a pause, the travel agent said, "I think Delta has some of the most wonderful people working for it, but those people evidence from time to time a frustration over the fact that they do not have the state of the art in the software reservation area. More importantly, I feel that Delta is a company which has a great sales force, but no marketing skills whatsoever."

After I confessed to being confused about the difference between sales and marketing, the travel agent replied, "Well, Delta can sell its service all day long, which it does very effectively, but basically, it is selling its timetable—'We can get you from here to there more efficiently,' etc., but what it doesn't have is an overall marketing strategy. I would define a marketing strategy as one where the sales representative calling on me would tell me why I should own Datas II or lease Datas II as opposed to why I should not have System One or some other carrier's computerized reservations system.

The fact is that a marketing strategy is a strategy which tells you why you are better than the other guy and the benefits and rewards that I will get from using your package as opposed to anybody else's. Delta just doesn't do that, and I regret it because so many of my people prefer to fly Delta, given a choice."

I then asked the agent what software system she used in her agency. She replied, "I use, first of all, Sabre, because there is nothing like it. A man can call up and book a flight for his wife to Honolulu and under the same entry in the computer, I can order a dozen orchids sent to her room when she gets to her hotel, not to mention the fact that in the meantime the same system has booked her hotel, her seat number, her return, her rental car, her tour, whatever else you care to name that goes along with the idea of traveling to Hawaii. I do, however, have a Datas II system, but use it only as a backup for those diehard passengers who use Delta almost exclusively, at least to the extent they can."

This travel agent obviously liked Delta, but seemed frustrated by Delta's inability or unwillingness to meet the strong competition head-on. I asked her to explain further. "It's not unwillingness at all," she said adamantly, "but a lack of resources or direction from the marketing offices of the company."

She said her typical traveler was an individual on business or a couple over the age of 40. Travelers who have come to Atlanta or have been here a long time and have felt that being part of the Atlanta community means being a loyal Delta fan.

"What about the dual-income-no-kids (DINKS) young couples that travel on a discretionary basis?" I asked her.

Without hesitating, she said, "We get very few young people flying on Delta. Their discounts are not competitive and are so confusing that not only can I not sell them very well, I don't even try. I feel that is unfortunate, because if Delta were more competitive in some of the discount fares, I would certainly steer business their way.

"In fact," she continued, "I don't remember the last time that Delta published a discount fare which was either competitive or understandable."

Survey of Travel Agents

My discussions with the Atlanta travel agent generated two surveys by two independent consulting firms based in Atlanta. Neither of the two firms knew until afterwards that the other had been conducting a related survey for the same client. Both surveys were national in scope and dealt with large, medium and smaller agencies.

The first was a general survey which polled travel agents regarding their preferences for airlines and for computerized software systems used in the booking of reservations. They were also asked to characterize attitudes of marketing representatives of the various airlines with whom they dealt.

The second survey was limited to obtaining opinions of travel agents on Datas II, why the agencies would or would not use the system and, if agencies used Datas II, what they liked best and what they liked least about it when they used it.

The general survey confirmed the feeling of the Atlanta travel agent with a pro-Delta bias: a sense of frustration in working with Delta, but a high regard for the service of the company, and a low regard for the Datas II product. Some agencies, however, were not so charitable, particularly off-line agencies, that is, those agencies that are located in certain cities that Delta does not serve directly. Similarly, smaller agencies felt that Delta generally ignores them, even if they are located in cities that Delta serves.

Even though both surveys were conducted independent of one another and in fact were both general in nature, they show results which are strikingly similar.[2] When a travel agency contracts with an airline to put in its computerized reservations system, it does so under a long-term lease agreement which is very costly to break prematurely to change to another system. Of the large travel agencies contacted, not one used Datas II as its primary system.

The owner of a large agency in California said that Delta had approached her some time ago, rather aggressively, about switching to Datas II. After reviewing the Delta proposal, she felt that Datas II was a good system—but not a significantly better system to warrant changing from her current system, PARS. In addition, the agent said that Delta was rigid about not helping by participating in the buy-out of the PARS lease as an incentive to buy Datas II. This observation was consistently made by every agency—large, medium and small—which had given some consideration to switching from another system to Datas II. The importance of this statement cannot be overemphasized; it reflects a rigidity on Delta's part that defies comprehension, given its last-place position in the computerized reservations system arena.

All the medium-sized agencies interviewed said they had been aggressively contacted by Delta to implement Datas II. A medium-sized agency in Tennessee has been using Datas II for several years. This agency expressed regrets about having switched to Datas II from the other systems (Sabre and Apollo) that she had used in the past. She rated Sabre the best and Datas II "... by far the worst." In this agent's views, Datas II was "... two years behind Sabre," and "... the quantity of information is less than the other systems, and there are fewer enhancements."

Of the small sized travel agencies interviewed, none have been approached by Delta to carry Datas II, but two had actually contacted Delta about Datas II and one of them decided to purchase it.

According to a principal of the agency that did not buy Datas II (but chose System One instead), Delta was not aggressive about selling its system. In fact, after the initial presentation was made, at the agency's request, Delta never contacted her again.

The agent indicated that there had been no incentive for its agency to purchase Datas II because Delta would not negotiate the price. Even though the company had approached Delta to seek reasons why it should purchase Datas II over PARS or System One, Delta still maintained an attitude of "take it or leave it." The same agency principal reported that she had heard from another travel agency that once Datas II is purchased, "... you will never hear from Delta again" and that Delta provides very little technical support or after-sale support on their system at all.

In conducting this survey, questions were also asked about fare incentives and frequent flyer programs. It is instructive to note that none of the agencies contacted discussed Delta when it came to the question of low fares or fare innovations. In addition, each agent mentioned that getting the lowest fare possible is more important to the leisure traveler than to someone going on business and that the business traveler is more concerned with accumulating frequent flyer points on their preferred airline and scheduling a convenient flight. Remember, Delta was three years later than American in instituting its frequent flyer program, which appears to be the only linchpin of consumer loyalty in the airline industry today. One of the survey's pluses, however, was that passengers reporting on their experience with Delta to the agencies consistently mentioned the good service they had from people who interacted directly with them, i.e., the Delta flight attendants.

Regardless of such rave reviews of Delta's service, when travel agencies control their passengers' choice of airlines, they rarely select Delta—and this is true of the agencies of every size. Delta does not seem to go out of its way to create good will in this critical segment of its market. For example, a large agency in Alabama observed that Delta will usually charge them for reservation errors, whereas other airlines typically do not. The manager of the agency complained: "That shows Delta makes a lot of money and can get away with it. But we don't like it, and it is chilling our relationship with them on an ongoing basis."

Similarly, the manager of a large travel agency in New York stated that she has a strong dislike of Delta because they offer absolutely no incentive to book passengers on the airline. Although competing carriers such as American and Eastern will give agents free trips, Delta has never made such an offer.

The smaller agencies consistently complained about neglect from Delta. The principal of a small agency in Oregon said that if she had a problem concerning Delta, she would not know whom to call. According to this agent, a Delta sales representative in San Francisco used to contact the agency at least once a month. At the time of the survey, however, it had been almost six months since she had heard from Delta, and they had even stopped sending her invitations to seminars that Delta puts on from time to time. She attributed this lack of attention to the fact that her shop was located in a small town which is not served by Delta.

Such neglect is not always limited to small travel agencies. A large travel agency in New York, which is, in fact, one of the largest in the United States, mainly books passengers on TWA, United and American because, they complained, "Delta is not very visible and rarely calls the agency to see how things are going." This agency has American's Sabre system in place, prefers American and its customers report that American's service, particularly to the West coast, is as good as the international carriers flying overseas.

Not all agencies contacted were critical about Delta's service and computerized reservations system. Another agent, a woman employed by a medium-sized agency in Tennessee that uses Datas II, reported that she frequently books clients on Delta and that the local representatives keep the agency well informed of any changes and are very willing to help with problems. But she did add that Datas II is not a competitive system; if she were to do it over again, the agency might not buy into Datas II.

The principal of a medium-sized agency in North Carolina contended that Delta's people are extremely responsive to her problems and the personnel in reservations are straightforward, give straight answers and are quick to respond. She had no complaints about the airline, but, interestingly enough, she did not use Datas II because she did not think it was competitive with System One.

The proprietor of a small travel agency in Missouri reported that Delta is her favorite airline because the people are very friendly and warm, and there is a consistency in the performance of the people working for the airline. However, she does not like Datas II, and in her agency uses System One instead. As a result, she works with Eastern the most. She claims that Eastern provides more revenue per ticket for the agency, and as most of her clients leave it to her as to what airline to choose, she invariably selects Eastern.

One of the principals of a large agency in New York reported that 75 percent of her bookings are business travelers who specify a definite preference for an airline due to the frequent flyer program. As a result, she remarked, she booked on American, United and TWA most often and that Delta was a distant—and she emphasized *distant*—fourth. She reported that until lately the best thing she liked about Delta was confidence in their service; things least liked were Delta's incentives to agencies and the inadequacy of the Datas II system.

The owner of a large travel agency in Sacramento, California commented that, "It was not practical to consider Datas II" because it is so inferior to PARS. He was troubled by the fact that the local sales people "... have no pull to fix screw-ups, the sales people cannot solve any problems." When asked if this might be due to the fact that Delta had recently merged with Western and that his city in particular was affected by the merger, he responded, "No, it has always been this way, Delta has too much centralized management. They need to delegate more work on a regional basis."

Unfortunately, the surveys were conducted during the months of July and August of 1987, when Delta had a multitude of operational problems, including a near miss over the Atlantic, the shutdown of the engines of a Boeing B-767 over the Pacific and, on several occasions, landings at wrong airports. Therefore, a number of the responses were biased against Delta because of a growing feeling that there were operational problems within the airline, so that a number of passengers were asking to be put on other airlines. The latter was probably a very short-term reaction for Delta.

The Second Survey

The second survey was undertaken specifically to obtain the travel agencies' opinions of Datas II. No categorization of agency by size was attempted; instead, the effort was directed to a much more random selection of agencies. Following is a summary of the comments that were received on Datas II from agencies outside of Atlanta:

• "Haven't seen Datas II. Heard it's up and coming, though technically well behind Sabre and Apollo. Only know one agency that uses it." (Kansas City PARS user.)

• "Probably good for a smaller agency because it is cheaper, although not for an agency as large as ours." (A Chicago Sabre user.)

• "Datas is trying hard to come up to the level of Sabre and Apollo, and they may make it. They don't have enhancements that others have." (Dallas Sabre user.)

• "Use only Datas II for boarding passes for passengers who booked it through themselves and then want the ticket delivered to their office. Delta won't deliver tickets, they just mail them. We only use it [Datas II] for a backup and have only one terminal. It will preprint Delta boarding passes." (Dallas primary Sabre user and secondary user of Datas II, which it got the month before the survey.)

• "Some of our offices use Datas II. Sabre can't bring up a Delta seat map and I need Datas II when a passenger calls for a certain seat number." (Dallas Sabre user.)

• "Worked on Datas II for a short time. Datas II was hard to work on because it was harder to reformat and everything had to be retyped verbatim. Short of codes and formats are too large. Could have gotten Datas II cheaper, but felt American's was better." (Sabre user in Dallas.)

- "Looked at Datas II, but as of two years ago it was not sophisticated enough, and we did more bookings with American." (Dallas Sabre user.)

Note that the last three agencies surveyed were Dallas agencies, the home office of American Airlines. They all used Sabre—American's system.

Consider what the following Atlanta travel agencies had to say about Delta's Datas II:

- "Does not have the enhancements and doesn't have the capabilities. Probably the worst system in the country. Delta will probably catch up. Only on the market four or five years. Will take some time to catch up. I don't know if they have hit the peak of Sabre, but they'll come up some." (Atlanta Sabre user.)

- "Datas II system not as good and different [from System One], which means staff retraining. Not worth it for us to change." (Atlanta System One user.)

- "Didn't choose Delta because it was not as sophisticated: Eastern gave us a better pricing arrangement and the in-house accounting system that we have does not interface with Delta's reservations system. Delta is not interested now in interfacing with non-Delta accounting systems." (Atlanta System One user.)

- "There is a lot of down time with Datas II. We use it on a secondary basis only for last-seat availability." (Atlanta System One user, primarily; Datas II only on a secondary basis.)

- "Improved. A lot more to it than used to be but you must consider that the airlines have all made drastic changes, and there are significant gaps in Datas II. May have to switch to Eastern or Continental." (Atlanta Datas II user.)

- "I did not want Datas II. I worked on it three years ago and found it extremely frustrating. Needed too many commands. I understand it may have improved, but really don't know." (Atlanta System One user.)

• "We chose Datas II four years ago over Eastern because Delta gave us a better presentation. Only Delta and Eastern were interested in the small agencies then .... Datas II has too much down time, and it needs too many enhancements, many of which should have been taken care of before they put the system on the market, but I really can't judge." (Atlanta Datas II user.)

From the perspective of travel agencies surveyed, Delta is not even faring well on its own home turf. However, most of the travel agencies interviewed in Atlanta volunteered the fact that they think Delta is a good company to work with. Moreover, because it is based in Atlanta, they prefer to work with Delta. Even so, they still don't use Delta's reservations system.

Consider the chart on the next page which shows the number of computer reservations systems installed by the airlines as of September 1986 and November 1987.

The situation is getting worse for Delta, not better. Delta is losing ground in the computerized reservations systems marketplace, not gaining it.   In the fourteen months from September 1986 until November 1987, American had signed up over   900 new travel agency subscribers for Sabre, whereas Delta had added a mere 232. How serious are the computerized reservations system owners about their systems? Some telling figures released by the Department of Transportation in mid-1988 are very revealing. For example, those figures reveal that computer reservations systems vendors (airlines) paid $42 million in cash in 1986 to induce subscribers to use their systems. Of that total, $3 million was paid by PARS, Apollo paid $6.1 million; Sabre paid $2.5 million, System One paid $3.2 million and Delta's Datas II paid only a paltry $698,000.

Through October 1986, Sabre (American) also provided *$142.4 million* in such non-cash incentives as free travel, hotel accommodations, seminars, luncheons and equipment discounts. Non-cash incentives provided by all other vendors together totaled less than $10 million.

The results are clear.

COMPUTER RESERVATIONS SYSTEMS

(Market Shares in 1986 and 1987)

Largest U.S. Airline Reservations Systems Worldwide Operations as of September 1986 and November 1987.

Number of Travel Agents Connected Worldwide

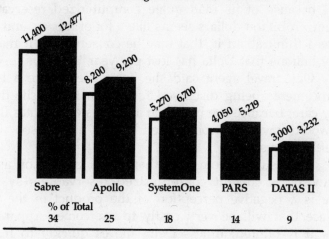

	Sabre	Apollo	SystemOne	PARS	DATAS II
% of Total	34	25	18	14	9

Number of Terminals Connected Worldwide

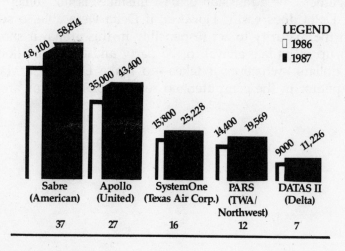

LEGEND
☐ 1986
■ 1987

	Sabre (American)	Apollo (United)	SystemOne (Texas Air Corp.)	PARS (TWA/ Northwest)	DATAS II (Delta)
	37	27	16	12	7

Source: Travel Weekly

According to *Aviation Daily*, in 1986, Sabre achieved 269 conversions of agencies from other systems, 1,378 new agency automations and 3,730 contract renewals. In contrast, Datas II converted only 87, automated only 349 and renewed 1,186.[3]

A former American Airlines marketing executive estimates that Delta has lost "billions of revenue each year since 1983" because of its inadequate computerized reservations system. "A billion dollars seems like a lot of money, and it is, but as I think about it, that may be conservative. It may be many billions that Delta has lost per year," he says.

One travel agent said she knew there were a lot of enhancements being discussed for Datas II, but she didn't really care, because she had such a bad taste for Datas II that she would have to be persuaded beyond any reason worth the effort to use it.

Delta suffers from more than just a lack of sophistication with its current computerized reservations system. There is a negative perception of the product in the marketplace that will be very costly to overcome. Apparently, Datas II is tainted; unless Delta moves quickly to restore confidence in the system, it might be better to scrap it altogether. The admission of past mistakes is not something that Delta does easily. However, if Delta were able to summon the maturity to act responsibly in this arena, it should own up to its late arrival to the party and begin to allocate the dollars—whatever it takes—to make Datas II a viable competitor in the computerized reservations systems arena.

Chapter Four

Fare Wars

"If you want to cut your own throat
don't come to me for a bandage."
—Margaret Thatcher

The Yield Managers

As we have seen, the ability to place an airline-specific computerized reservations system within travel agencies and thereby promote ticket sales has become the single most important external activity in the airline business. Similarly, the most important internal activity of an airline is management of its yields. It is difficult to over-emphasize the importance of yield management since deregulation; in short, it is not just the name of the game, it may very well *be* the whole game.

In its most basic sense, "yield" is the amount of revenue-dollars an airline gets per revenue-passenger-mile. Non-paying passengers, such as airline employees flying on passes, do not count. In effect, the size of yield depends on how effective the airline is at moving the seats its customers have paid to occupy. An airline that manages its yield poorly is destined to suffer an erosion of earnings, if, indeed, not sustain tremendous operating losses.

A Definition

Dr. James describes yield management as "A core of pricing by computer experienced personnel constantly changing fare levels based on the seasons, the phase of the business cycle, the changing numbers and strategies of competitors, the amount of advanced bookings, the type and availability of aircraft and seats and other related factors—all with the objective of maximizing revenue on every flight."[1]

Obviously, the better that the management of an airline manages its yield, which is essentially the percentage of every dollar which represents profit from the movement of passengers per revenue mile, the better chances it has for turning a profit. The significance of yield can be demonstrated by the fact that if one passenger fare per flight were changed from a discount fare to a full fare, in Delta's case it would add over $52 million per year in additional revenue.[2]

The New Samurais

The fare wars have wrought havoc on airline yields in the past few years, and there is no indication that in the long term this punishing condition will decrease. It is almost as if fares were being invented by a new kind of manager who regularly throws caution to the wind and attempts to gain market share at any cost. This new Samurai mentality seems to owe more to the tradition of berserk warriors charging into battle bent on destruction of the enemy at any cost, than to the tradition of calm, computer-managed logistics supposedly typical of the modern MBA-trained manager. Obviously, deteriorating yields have a deteriorating impact on earnings, and high-cost carriers such as Delta remain extremely vulnerable to the inability of the industry to price its services profitably. Perhaps it is the smell of this vulnerability which drives these new Samurais into their havoc-for-havoc's-sake mode.

Yields in the fourth quarter of 1985 for the U.S. scheduled airlines were 11.8 cents per mile. By the end of the fourth quarter of 1986, they had dropped to 10.8 cents per mile. In other words, the industry went from revenues of 11.8 to 10.8 cents per dollar of revenue in just a years' time, a decline of 8.5 percent.

Delta's yield, over the same time, declined from 14.5 cents to 13.1 cents per mile—a 9.7 percent decline which was 40 percent more than the industry's. Delta's yield for fiscal 1987 ending June 30, 1987 declined again to 12.81 cents, reflecting at the time a steadily deteriorating yield.

Delta's pattern of hesitance held true to form, and Delta waited nearly three years after American established its yield management department before it formed one of its own in July of 1983.

In an effort to counter the yield management problems brought on by the discount fares, many scheduled airlines attempted in 1986 to put a strong hold on employee costs. As a result, the 1986 average cost per employee compensation dropped steadily in each of the four quarters—from $43,200 in the first quarter to only $41,600 in the fourth quarter. Delta countered the trend again, and its annual compensation per employee rose, from the end of 1986, 1.6 percent—from $49,264 to $50,060.

The Continental Threat

The Lorenzo-managed Continental Airlines, after re-emergence from bankruptcy, continues to pay significantly less annual compensation per employee than the older established carriers such as Delta. Continental's compensation average for the year ending 1986 was $27,700 versus an industry average for the older carriers of $43,500, a difference of $15,800.

What is the significance of this difference in compensation if one is discussing the effect of yield on a particular carrier's profitability? The short and simple answer is that Continental can live with a substantially lower yield than the older established carriers and, in particular, Delta.

It becomes instructive, therefore, to compare Continental's yield versus Delta's yield in their top 50 markets. At first blush, this seems somewhat irrelevant since Continental and Delta compete very little on a head-to-head basis nowadays, except for certain route segments acquired by Delta when it purchased Western.

However, one of the curses or blessings of deregulation, depending on whom you are talking to, is the ability of the management of one airline holding company which owns more than one airline to move its airplanes or airlines from city to city or hub to hub on a selected basis. Nowhere is this ability more potentially devastating than in Atlanta, where Eastern and Delta have a virtual strangle hold as they control 90 percent of the air traffic operations. As a result,

these two carriers have historically kept fares artificially
inflated to the perpetual detriment of the traveler, particularly the business traveler. The matter is further exacerbated
by the fact that Atlanta is a large hub operation for both
Eastern and Delta, which have inherent fare penalties for
passengers who must travel to or through them because of
operational schedules.

Deregulation War Games

It is not difficult to imagine what might happen if Frank
Lorenzo, in an effort to garner an increased market share
out of Atlanta, were to impose Continental's yields on Eastern. If, however, Lorenzo is not successful in settling his
battles with Eastern's unions, he might very well choose to
dismantle the airline altogether and replace it with Continental, the lowest cost operator in the industry. If Delta were to
face Continental's yields on its home turf in Atlanta, it would
be nothing short of calamitous for the company.

The illustration on the following page compares the
yields of Continental and Delta in each of the carriers' top 50
markets for the second quarter of 1986. For all flights of
more than 1,000 miles within the continental United States,
the yields for both Continental and Delta are essentially the
same. Surprisingly, in some cases they are actually lower on
Delta. For flights of less than 1,000 miles, however, Continental yields are substantially lower than Delta's yields. This
fact becomes especially meaningful when it is considered
that Delta's average length of each trip within the Continental United States was only 572 miles before the Western
acquisition and still only 610 miles afterwards. In addition,
33 of Delta's top 50 domestic markets are easily below 1,000
miles. Moreover, all but one of these 33 top domestic markets had higher yields than Continental.

If we break these 33 markets into three separate units
of 0-450 miles, 450-650 and 650-1000 miles, respectively, then
some interesting relationships are exposed. In markets
below 450 miles, Delta's yields were approximately 66 percent higher than Continental's, while in markets within the
450-650 mile category, Delta yields were approximately 50

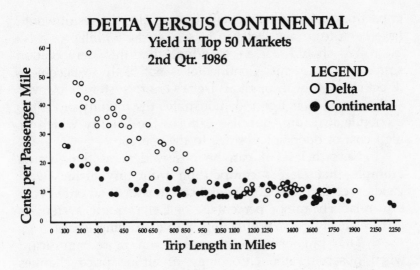

DELTA VERSUS CONTINENTAL
Yield in Top 50 Markets
2nd Qtr. 1986

LEGEND
○ **Delta**
● **Continental**

Cents per Passenger Mile

Trip Length in Miles

Yield:
(¢ /Revenue Passenger Mile)

percent higher. But in markets within the 650-1,000-mile trip lengths, Delta's yields were roughly 33 percent higher.[3]

Let's say that the Lorenzo-managed Continental had gone after Delta during the second quarter of 1986 and concentrated only on Delta's markets out of Atlanta. At that time, revenue from this segment of Delta's markets represented 6.3 percent of Delta's entire system revenue. If, however, Lorenzo had forced Delta to compete head-to-head with Continental's pricing during this same period and, as a result, forced Delta to realize Continental's substantially lower yields, Delta's Atlanta revenue would have been 3.3 percent of its entire system, for a 48 percent reduction in total revenue. This would have reduced Delta's revenue by $51.2 million per quarter, or nearly $206 million for the fiscal year. Further, the impact of such competition—*in this Atlanta arena only*—would have caused Delta's 1986 operating profitability to plummet from $225 million to a mere $6 million!

If, on the other hand, Lorenzo challenged Delta across its entire route system, and if we assume the same impact because of Continental's lower yield, the result would have been to drown Delta in losses of over $3 billion.

We should hasten to admit that this deregulation scenario is academic: Continental is not likely to become a direct competitor throughout Delta's entire system. However, such a scenario not only demonstrates the fragility of Delta's economic structure, but also exposes the liability which its high cost of operations brings to the company.

Nevertheless, it can be observed from the Atlanta example that Delta's competition from any airline with yields such as those Continental can muster need only occur in a relatively minor percentage of Delta's route system to turn relatively good profitability into disturbing losses.

This phenomenon becomes even more significant when observing the chronology of airline price changes beginning in early 1987 that shows Continental as the strongest price leader in the industry. Such leadership might easily be expected from a company such as Texas Air Corporation, which:

- serves more cities than any other U.S. airline;
- has the largest number of hubs; and
- possesses both the lowest labor costs and the lowest unit cost structure of any large airline in the industry.

Two Scenarios of Competition

Even with severe price competition, a quality carrier can mount quite an attack. Witness the 1983 encounter between the renewed Braniff and American Airlines, when Braniff challenged American in its Dallas market. American did not hesitate to match Braniff's extraordinarily low fares. American sustained operating losses, but it continued to hold its market share out of Dallas. Braniff could not sustain the attack and was finally forced to scale down.

A similar situation occurred in the Denver market in the Fall of 1983, when Continental Airlines went into receivership. When it emerged from bankruptcy with costs now greatly reduced, it challenged United with reduced fares— fares which United failed to match. As a result, United suffered a major loss of its market share, while Continental recouped a large portion of the Denver market it had held prior to bankruptcy proceedings. Continental walked away from the contest as a serious, long-run, low-cost, large competitor.

One of the issues that shrouds the airline industry today is passenger loyalty. Do passengers really care what airline they fly if they can get to their destination at a preferred time and at a competitive price?

According to Steve Rothmeier, chairman of Northwest, "there's no brand loyalty in this business" because in the classic sense, customers who defect to another carrier because of poor service usually return after only a short time.[4]

This view is supported by comments from frequent flyers. One such flyer is William Pratt, who travels about 100,000 miles a year. "It means little to me if there are more or less complaints about an airline," says Pratt, a Chicago lawyer. "I'll take Continental without batting an eye if it has the most convenient schedule."[5]

Says Ronald Nelson, who flies often as the Purchasing Director of TRW, Inc., it doesn't matter which carrier he takes because "there's no one airline that gives outstanding service."[6] Since deregulation, airline marketers have been slow to learn how to build distinct identities in the marketplace. If airline passengers can be obtained and held at a price, even if it is just a question of how much, then trouble is on the horizon for the Delta management which has repeatedly asserted it will not sacrifice service, obtained with very high operating costs, on the altar of deregulation.

Capacity Liability

Delta currently has more airliners and hence more capacity on order and option than any other carrier in the country. This will be a distinct advantage if business volume holds or improves. If volume declines, however, rolling additional capacity into the system becomes a liability. The result is that there are too many empty seats in the sky—so load factors drop, profitability declines and losses occur.

Following almost six years of extraordinary financial health in this country, Americans are poised in late 1988 on the edge of an uncertain economic future. If a recession or mild slowdown occurs in the economy, air travel will be substantially reduced. Discretionary travel (vacations) could be virtually eliminated, and business travel, which contributes a significant percentage of revenue for Delta and in fact most airlines, will be significantly affected.

As we will see, Delta's controllable costs continue to escalate as they have throughout this decade. Consequently, its profit margins are eroding, and at some point large gross revenues will no longer mask constantly rising costs. With this gamble on increased capacity, Delta is clearly courting financial disaster.

Delta's Vulnerability is Unmanaged and Unyielding

Today, it is fair to say that Delta manages its yield better than some but not as effectively as the best. Regardless of these skills, the company's cost infrastructure continues to expose it to a competitive onslaught by either Continental or a revitalized Eastern. Delta will not withstand either challenge effectively unless it is willing to sustain large losses, or alternatively, slash costs, principally through labor reduction. My guess is that it will not have either the strength of character or the wisdom to choose correctly in charting a course around these economic shoals.

---------------- Chapter Five ----------------

Delta's Illusory Management Style

"Even a blind chicken can find
a grain of corn now and again."
—anonymous

Economic Cost Cutting at Delta

In January of 1980, Delta had yet to encounter the economic turbulence of later periods, but even then the company was making noises about cutting costs. They were noises which had, however, a curiously hollow sound to them. Its ideas of serious savings consisted of:

• Using cloth headrest covers instead of paper ones because it is less costly to launder cloth covers than to keep buying paper ones;

• Cutting the number of shrimp in a shrimp cocktail to four from five;

• Vacuuming its planes more frequently to reduce the weight of jets;

• Requiring workers in departments to use their pencils down to two inches before getting new ones; and

• Requiring executives to save the paper clips that arrived with each day's mail and to uses them instead of buying their own.

A Delta public relations spokesman was actually heard to brag, "We have zero paper clip attrition."[1] If this is representative of the quality of fiscal management and cost containment at Delta in fairly good times, then one is forced to wonder what kind of inventive cutbacks will be summoned when Delta is in serious trouble. More to the point is a larger question about the general quality of fiscal management at Delta. If we look at the facts, I am convinced, we discover that current management practices fall far short of expectations. In an industry as challenged by deregulation as is the airline industry, the management of a company's finances cannot afford to be afraid of hard choices.

Airlines: A Poor Investment

As a general proposition, investments in airlines during this decade have been poor ones at best. As we have seen, the current and historic profitability of the airlines through the period of deregulation simply does not justify the existing levels of investment, nor can these kinds of profits justify investments of a similar nature in the future. Further, the balance sheets of the industry are so overloaded with debt that in order to service such debt the industry is, literally, slowly liquidating itself.

And no wonder. As the following chart illustrates, the 1984 return on investment for the S&P 400 industrial companies was a healthy 5.88 percent. For the same year, the Standard & Poor's return on investment in the U.S. airline industry was a mere 2.23 percent—and that was the best year to date in this decade for the airline industry in terms

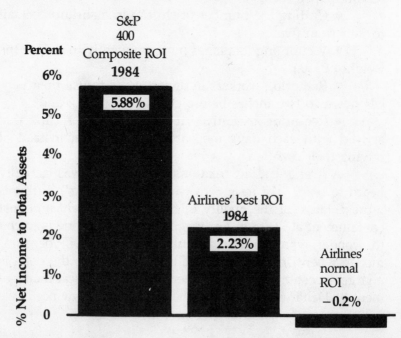

of profitability. Moreover, the normal rate of return for the airline industry in this decade (through 1986) has been a -0.2 percent. No industry can sustain such numbers for very long and remain viable.

Delta: An Inconsistent Player at Best

Delta's financial performance compared with the performance of other major carriers through 1986 as defined by Standard & Poor's is revealing. The only consistency in Delta's financial performance during this decade is its inconsistency.[2]

Even when the deck is stacked by the inclusion of such poor profit performers as Continental, Trans World and Pan American in the composite, Delta still does not fare well in a comparison done by Standard and Poor's.

It should be noted Standard & Poor's examines several key ratios to determine Delta's position as compared to the *Airline Composite Index* through 1986. These key ratios were:

● return on assets (an asset efficiency measure);
● return on equity (a performance measure);
● current ratios (asset to debt, a measure of the firm's liquidity);
● debt to capital (a measure of leverage).

Of these key ratios, only Delta's return on assets and equity were substantially above those of the airlines compared prior to 1986. In 1986, however, all four of these ratios dropped dramatically. See the table on the following page.

For example, Delta's return on assets plunged from 7.5 percent in 1985 to 1.3 percent in 1986. During the same period, the composite dropped only from 3.0 percent to 1.4 percent. Delta's return on equity showed an even larger fall, from 22.2 percent in 1985 to only 3.7 percent in 1986. During the same period, the competition's key ratios fell from 8.8 percent to 4.2 percent. The following table sets this forth on a comparative analysis:

	Return on Assets		
	1984	**1985**	**1986***
Delta	5.4%	7.5%	1.3%
Composite	3.5%	3.0%	1.4%

	Return on Equity		
	1984	**1985**	**1986**
Delta	18.0%	22.2%	3.7%
Composite	9.7%	8.8%	4.2%

	Current Ratio		
	1984	**1985**	**1986**
Delta	0.6	0.7	0.8
Composite	1.0	1.1	0.9

	Debt to Capital		
	1984	**1985**	**1986**
Delta	30.4%	22.0%	31.6%
Composite	52.4%	54.7%	58.0%

*S&P 1987 composite not available.

Recent regional studies point up dramatic decline. Of the top 50 non-financial companies in Georgia, Delta was sixth in revenue and sixth in net income in 1988, according to *Georgia Trend* magazine's July 1988 issue. On the same list, however, Delta is 47th in its return on equity and falls completely off the chart which measures return on assets.[3]

Delta has not purchased a new aircraft since 1984. Instead, the company has opted for financial leasing from The Boeing Company and the McDonnell-Douglas Corporation through a number of financial institutions. As a consequence, Delta is not in an acquisition mode which would increase assets on the balance sheet; it is, instead, pursuing an active program of selling aircraft and, in effect, liquidating assets. Although Delta's current balance sheet is, for the moment, one of the healthiest in the airline industry, without compensating additions this liquidation of assets program will in time have a debilitating effect.

Delta's Operating Expenses Examined

Throughout the '80s there has been tremendous volatility in Delta's total operating expenses. Total operating costs as a percent of total revenues have ranged from a high of 105.7 percent in 1983, when the company lost $2.18 per share with an operating loss of $5.21 per share, to a low of 92.2 percent in 1985. As we shall see, operating expenses continue to move upward *if consistent accounting standards are applied.*

For purposes of the following analyses, operating costs were separated into two very basic categories— controllable and uncontrollable. This pair of categories allows for an analysis and assessment of how well the management of the company has influenced, or indeed, controlled expenses. Some of the expenses defined as "uncontrollable," that is, not capable of being reduced or eliminated in the short term, include:

- fuel and
- landing fees.

Expenses that are defined as "controllable" are those over which management exercises discretion and which could be reduced or eliminated on short notice; these include:

- salaries;
- aircraft maintenance materials;
- repairs;
- aircraft lease costs and other rent;
- passenger service costs;
- passenger service commissions and other cash costs; and
- depreciation and amortization.

Delta's controllable expenses have rocketed from 67.88 percent of revenue in 1980 to 81.68 percent for fiscal year 1987. Delta's management continues to demonstrate its persistent inability to come to grips with this potentially deadly issue. The following chart graphs Delta's controllable and uncontrollable expenses expressed as a percentage of total revenues for each year from 1980 through 1988.

While fuel expense comprises the great portion of uncontrollable costs, these costs did, mercifully, drift lower through 1987. On the other hand, however, controllable expenses moved up dramatically from 1980 through 1987 and the underlying trend is projected clearly upward. Therefore, in spite of dollar amounts of revenues, unless Delta can do something to bring down its margin of expenses relative to revenues, there is some inevitable point out there on the horizon—if Delta's management continues its lackluster performance—when expenses will outpace revenues. At that point, Delta's financial picture will take a dramatic turn for the worse.

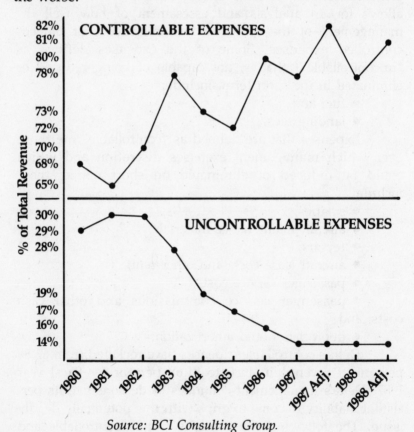

Source: BCI Consulting Group.

Welfare State at Delta

THE FATAL NO-LAYOFF POLICY

What has really eroded the sinew of Delta's muscle is its inability to control its wage costs, the largest component in the controllable segment of its expenses. Without an inspired maneuver which defuses its rigid no-layoff wage policy, this explosive segment of the overhead will give Delta its *coup de grace*.

Robert Oppenlander, Delta's chief financial officer for nearly 30 years, was a strong vocal supporter of Delta's long-time policy of never laying off permanent workers. Such inflexible policy dictates payroll costs which stymie Delta's ability to act swiftly in an economic downturn and to deal effectively with the problem of what to do with a full work force when passenger volume is falling. No financial officer at Delta, let alone any structural mechanism, can challenge the policy that there should be no deviation from Delta's tradition of continuous generosity to its employees in good times or in bad.

"Once you are committed to a welfare state," says an executive of a competing carrier in regard to Delta's no-layoff policy, "the marginal cost of using your labor is very low, so you might as well fly. In the long term, that could kill you, but it's not a bad short-term approach to life and can help you keep your market share."

Delta may have waited too long, and have been too generous to derive the kind of mature loyalty from its employees that the policy was designed to generate. One retired staff director at Delta says that the Delta employees "... are like spoiled children. They have grown used to substantial pay increases on an annual basis. Once it is realized that the annual pay raises have been taken away from them, they will be no different than stereotyped airline employees. They will be surly and otherwise uncooperative and indifferent."

A TOKEN REMEDY, AND ITS EFFECT

Delta has made a token effort to transform its policy of annual pay raises by substituting the cost-of-living index for annual merit wage increases. In addition, they have begun awarding only occasional bonuses to the entire work force, bonuses which are later not included in compensation calculations for purposes of computing retirement benefits.

This fact has not gone unnoticed among Delta employees, particularly at the mid-range management and professional level where a typical employee is in his 40s and beginning to see darkness at the end of that tunnel called a "career path." As a result, resumes of Delta managers and professionals are now circulating in the marketplace as never before. To be sure, many have succumbed to solicitations from outside firms, but according to sources inside Delta, there has never been an occasion when so many Delta employees were actively looking for jobs on their own. Delta has already lost a number of talented young professionals who have felt stifled and hence have opted for more stimulating environments elsewhere.

What is the import of continued high wages at Delta, as it faces increasing competition on its home turf and the strong possibility of substantially reduced fares in the Southeast which this competition will generate? An illustration of these potential problems is seen at Nashville and Raleigh-Durham, where "service-conscious" American Airlines has recently established large hub operations. The focus on Atlanta as the axis of travel to the Southeast is already being drained by the combination of strong competition from American and United and the very strong challenge from USAir and Piedmont.[4]

"They're going to have to cope with a level of competition they haven't faced before," says Donald Lloyd-Jones, former president of Western Air Lines. "Delta may be at a severe disadvantage if Texas Air Corp's chairman, Frank Lorenzo, succeeds in reincarnating Eastern as a low-cost carrier. Allen [chairman and CEO of Delta] would have a hard time slashing the company's high wages without disrupting the loyal, service-minded, family-like culture that has been nurtured carefully throughout Delta's 60-year history."[5]

Not everyone agrees with this assessment, however. Salomon Brothers' respected airline analyst Julius Maldutis thinks that price alone is not as important as quality of service. Although fares will continue to influence travelers, there's little doubt that the quality of airline service is growing in importance. "We may be entering a new phase where few, if any, price differentials exist. Now it'll be on service."[6]

If Maldutis is correct, then Delta will undoubtedly be a big winner—but in this instance he may well be wrong. There is convincing evidence that pricing will ultimately be the sole criterion for the discretionary traveler, while for the business traveler pricing and convenience will be of equal importance.

Assuming that this analysis is half correct, fares will in fact continue to influence travelers, and service will remain a big issue as well. The question is whether Delta can do two things:

● First, can Delta slash fares? This is something it must do to match the fares that American, Eastern and Continental are going to charge in the Southeast.

● Secondly, can Delta slash wages? If it is to offer competitive fares and at the same time operate profitably then wages have to be reduced.

WHAT IF HARD TIMES CAME TO DELTA?

Let's assume that Delta's employees were forced to take a wage reduction of as much as 50 percent in order to compete with Continental and a somewhat less substantial reduction in order to compete with American. Would Delta still be able to offer high quality service by motivated employees?

If human nature prevails, the answer must be an unqualified "No!" Delta openly acknowledges that it gets quality service and keeps the unions at bay only by paying a premium in salaries, so the question may be academic.

There is some recent evidence, however, to suggest that this question may not be so academic after all, and that Delta's lofty position as the highest-cost operator in the business is not fully appreciated by many of its employees.

On July 6, 1988 Delta announced that it was giving its non-union employees their first "real" pay raises in three years, ranging from 3 to 5 percent of salary. "There has been a lot of grumbling because we knew we were making a lot of money," said one worker who did not want to be named. "It was tough for the older employees, because we were used to getting raises every year. This was the longest we had ever gone without a raise."[7]

Those having less seniority were disgruntled, too. Said one mechanic, who also did not wish to be identified, "skilled workers on the B-Scale[8] are getting impatient with Delta. We have a lot of B-Scale mechanics who are going to United Parcel Service to become airplane mechanics because they are getting tired of this."[9]

It would appear that Delta is in a no-win situation. That its workers may know Delta is the highest-cost operator in the industry—that doesn't seem to concern them so long as it is their ox that is being gored. Perhaps the allegation that Delta's employees are like spoiled children was not entirely inappropriate. Only time will assess the maturity of Delta's work force and if, collectively, employees will be willing to make some sacrifices to help out a company that has been very good to them.

Following the July 1988 pay raises, however, something virtually unprecedented for Delta occurred. Later that month, The Teamsters Union started a drive to organize Delta's baggage handlers, targeting former Western employees as the most promising candidates for unionization. That is an incredible irony, since these people already benefit so substantially because of Delta's largess in bringing them up to Delta pay scales. Indeed, Delta has put them into salary and benefit plans they never dreamed of at Western.

William Geneose, Sr., head of the Airline Division of the Teamster's Union, said he believed that "... many Delta workers recently had become interested in joining a union because of unhappiness over their latest raises."[10] Geneose also believed that other Delta employees, such as the mechanics, might be susceptible to union activities by the International Association of Machinists and Aerospace Workers since the Union has an advantage because of the former Western workers.

In response to questions about recent union activities, Edward Starkman, an analyst with Paine Webber predicted the Teamsters would fail at Delta. "They have the highest average compensation in the business. I don't see what bringing in a union would do for them—other than cost them union dues," Starkman said.[11]

It makes one shudder to think what the reaction at Delta's work force would be if the company had to, in fact, slash its wages in order to stay competitive in this dynamic era of deregulation.

THE MYTH OF THE
PRODUCTIVE DELTA FAMILY EXPLODED!

Historically, Delta has been completely unsuccessful in dealing with employee compensation, at least in terms of managing it as an element of controllable expenses.

In 1986, the U.S. airline industry experienced its first annual drop in employee compensation, moving from an average of $43,200 per employee in 1985 to $42,200 in 1986. The trend continued in 1987. Of the major trunk airlines, only United and Delta bucked the trend.

United's annual compensation per employee in the same period increased a whopping 7.9% from $41,700 in 1985 to $44,988 in 1986. Still, on a dollar basis, it remained on a reasonable parity with American.

Delta's average annual compensation per employee in 1986, including wages, salaries, payroll taxes and fringe benefits increased 1.6 percent to $50,066 per employee, whereas American's decreased by 9.3 percent to $43,911 from $48,422. Similarly, Continental's declined from $30,339 to $28,499. Obviously, if Delta is to match the future fare cuts that are envisioned, then it has to at least stabilize its upward trend—if not try something even more drastic. It would be wise, for example, to bring the average compensation per Delta employee more closely in line with that of its strongest competitors—American and, certainly Continental —if possible.

These figures become even more meaningful if we examine the five-year trend from 1982 through 1986. If we analyze only wages but no other indirect forms of compensation, then in 1986, the average direct wage per employee at Delta was $48,529—versus $27,246 at Continental and $41,477 at American.

While this is not unexpected in light of the other 1986 data, what is surprising is the trend: in 1982 Delta's average direct compensation per employee was $39,920, at Continental it was $33,683 and at American $41,012. It is clear to see, then, that Delta has experienced an average increase of almost $9,000 per employee per direct compensation during the same period of time in which Continental's has actually decreased by over $6,000 per employee and American's has only risen by $300 per employee in the last four years.

Let's look at this another way. For each dollar of employee compensation American paid, it tallied 23,810 revenue passenger miles. Even more dramatically, Continental tallied an impressive 45,750, but Delta could count only 16,600. Therefore, Continental obtained almost three times the revenue for each dollar of employee compensation as Delta, while American obtained over one-and-a-half times more than Delta. These figures should put Delta's much-vaunted "employee productivity" argument to final rest. The myth of the highly productive "Delta Family," is just that— fiction!

The Bloated Delta Staff

The irrepressible chairman of the board who charted so much of Delta's current geography, Tom Beebe, told *Financial World* in 1978: "We're not just a good-weather airline. Some airlines can make money only in a good economy. We make money in good times and in bad times."[12]

The decade of the 1980s would prove Beebe wrong. Delta has not only made money in good times, it has also lost money in good times. Much of this ability to lose money in good times as well as bad is triggered by Delta's increasingly bloated staff.

For example, Delta's legal department boasts a staff as large today as it was ten years ago, when there were massive on-going proceedings before the Civil Aeronautics Board that would involve as many as seven lawyers at any one time. The legal department is not an isolated case. That bloat can be found throughout the company as seen in the case of the assistant treasurer who retired from the company in 1987 and was immediately put on a consulting contract to do some specialized work for Delta—for a fee in addition to his retirement pay. It has long been a joke that a job with Delta is security for life, providing you don't get caught sleeping with one of your employees.

THE OVERPAID WESTERN EMPLOYEES

When Delta acquired Western and moved several hundred of its former staff personnel from Los Angeles to Atlanta, it immediately put those former Western employees on the same wage scale that Delta was then currently paying. Delta completely overlooked the fact that these employees were going to receive a major one-time pay hike because the cost of living in Los Angeles is estimated to be as much as 20 percent higher than it is in Atlanta. Western employees did well by themselves, but whether it is in Delta's long-term interest to be so generous remains a serious question.

A startling example of Delta's largess towards Western is seen in the examination of a captain's pay for flying a variety of aircraft at several different airlines pre-and post-merger. [See the table on the following page.] It should be noted that Delta's 727 captains made 65 percent more than Western's 727 captains, and, of course, that the Western captains were immediately moved to the Delta scale. Given the same circumstances in other acquisitions, the resulting shift in the salary scales of other captains demonstrates that no other airline was so radical in that shift as Delta.

Impact of Mergers on Pilots' Pay

Merger	Aircraft type	Maximum captain hourly wages on June 1, 1987		
		Surviving airline	Merging airline	Percent difference
American/Air Cal	MD-80/ B737	126.62	99.29	27.5%
Delta/Western	B-727	143.33	86.81	65.1%
Northwest/Republic	B-727	139.23	87.26	59.6%
TWA/Ozark	MD-80	92.52	114.41	-65.1%
United/Pan Am Pacific	B-747	173.05	146.89	17.8%
USAir/PSA	DC-9	135.14	111.67	21.0%
USAir/Piedmont	B-727	139.36	138.39	0.87%

OVERPAID DELTA CAPTAINS

If we examine a captain's maximum annual pay for flying the largest aircraft at each airline, then we will see that Delta's is also the highest, paying on average $166,548 to captains who fly 75 hours a month.[13] As a result Delta pays those who pilot the L-1011, the largest aircraft in its fleet, more money than any other industry captain earns. [See the following table.]

Pilots' maximum pay

A captain's maximum annual pay for flying the largest aircraft at some of the nation's major airlines, and the number of flight hours per month on which the pay is based.

Airline	Flight hours per month	Maximum annual pay
Delta	75	$166,548
Northwest	75	$162,000
United	80	$161,976
American	75	$154,000
Eastern	86	$121,548
Pan Am	80	$115,000
Continental	83	$71,000
Major airline average	80	$136,843

Source: Future Aviation Professional of America

It is startling to note that Northwest and United, as the two carriers paying respectively, the next-highest maximum annual pay for captains, both operate four-engine B-747 aircraft. These aircraft are substantially heavier, have longer range and payload capabilities and are more technologically sophisticated than Delta's L-1011s. To further qualify this matter, United pays a B-747 captain a maximum annual pay of $161,976 for flying 80 hours a month, a far more efficient arrangement for United.

A more precise comparison of captains' pay can be made between American and Delta. American operates DC-10s, aircraft very similar to the L-1011 in terms of its performance, and yet American pays its DC-10 captains over $12,500 a year less than Delta L-1011 captains receive.

To put comparisons made with Continental into perspective, it should be noted that Continental's maximum pay, $71,000, is for captains flying former People Express B-747 aircraft to Europe. These captains make almost $100,000 a year less than Delta's captains and, in addition, fly more hours.

The Delta Vulnerability: Fuel Costs

DELTA'S FUEL BILL

Fuel is the major component of uncontrollable costs. Fuel costs have generally declined during this decade, though they showed a modest upturn during 1987.

While the following example uses Delta figures only, it would be grossly unfair not to admit that the risk of increased fuel costs is an industry-wide risk.

Since 1980, Delta's fuel costs have fallen from demanding a 29 percent share of total expenses in 1980 to only a 12.6 percent share of total expenses in 1987. However, while fuel costs decreased through 1987, Delta's other uncontrollable operating costs, such as landing fees, have gradually increased.

What does this mean? As a rule of thumb, the airline industry estimates that for every one penny per gallon that aviation fuel prices change, $1 million will be passed through to the bottom line of the profit-and-loss statement. If aviation fuel goes from 75 cents per gallon to 76 cents per gallon, then an additional $1 million in red ink crosses the loss statement. However, if the price falls from 75 cents per gallon to 74 cents then a savings of $1 million could be chalked up—or so the rule of thumb would indicate.

A more analytical approach to the impact on a particular carrier is determined by examining the total amount of fuel purchased and then determining the net effect per share. In 1986, Delta purchased 1,532,500,000 gallons of aviation fuel. If the price of fuel had fluctuated a mere one penny per gallon up or down, then there would have been a shift of $15.3 million in expenses, which would have resulted in a net effect of plus or minus 26 cents of earnings per share. Through the first quarter of 1988, fuel prices have started creeping gradually upwards, a fact which increased Delta's expenses for the end of its third quarter in fiscal 1988.

What if the problem were more severe? Using 1986 as a base,

- *IF* the U.S. Department of Commerce's early 1988 forecast was accurate and fuel oil prices began to increase at an average rate of 5 percent per year for the next ten years, and
- *IF* we assume, in addition, that Delta's basic fuel consumption rate remains the same, and
- *IF* fuel prices increase 50 cents per gallon
- *THEN* a negative effect of $1.30 per share on Delta's earnings would result in any year that these assumptions are applied.

Obviously, as consumption is increased through route expansion, and increases in flight frequencies, the whole scenario becomes exacerbated. If we apply this example to the earnings per share of Delta in any year of this decade, we will see that there could have been a dramatic change in Delta's profitability if fuel prices had not been stabilized. The inability of the OPEC ministers to hold their cartel in place has been the greatest stroke of luck which Delta has experienced during the '80s.

But OPEC is not the only threat which the airline industry might anticipate. The mercurial situation concerning oil prices is demonstrated by an accident that happened in July 1988, when a North Sea oil rig was totally destroyed by fire. The result of that single disaster was a rush on fuel crude prices which went up over $1 a barrel in one single day!

THE STRATEGIC VULNERABILITY OF DELTA

That Delta is strategically vulnerable is easily demonstrated by simply projecting the fuel costs for 1982 as if they had continued to be the same percent of total revenue that year, when fuel costs were 29.80 percent of revenue, down from their high of 30.28 percent the previous year.

Projecting the 1982 fuel costs as a percent of total revenues to the years 1983 through 1987 will produce an astonish-ing portrait of financial disaster.[14] If 1982 fuel costs had stabilized through 1983-1987 and all other costs continued to develop, as history has shown they did, then Delta would have experienced losses for each year. In addition, all

measurements of profitability would have dropped significantly. Net earnings before taxes, net earnings after taxes
and earnings per share would all have suffered large
declines.

For example, net earnings before taxes would have
been the most negatively influenced by the hypothetical
change in fuel costs. The largest percentage difference
would have occurred in 1986, when net earnings would have
reached a horrendous *negative 15,498 percent*! Left
unchecked, such trends would have produced in 1987 a
cataclysmic loss of $912,811,000. In this scenario, Delta
would have been a very dead issue long before the hemor-
rhage became so acute.

Net income after taxes also changed significantly,
although given the tax advantages which losses generate,
the change was not as dramatic as we saw in net earnings
before taxes:

NET EARNINGS BEFORE TAXES
WITH AND WITHOUT THE FUEL ADJUSTMENT

NEBT (Millions)	Year				
	1983	1984	1985	1986	1987
Actual Figures	(226,701)	240,215	405,163	3,434	447,199
Adjusted Figures	(305,238)	(92,188)	(98,521)	(528,781)	(465,612)
Difference	78,537	323,403	503,684	532,215	912,811
% Change	–35%	–138%	–124%	–15,498%	–204%

NET EARNINGS AFTER TAXES
WITH AND WITHOUT THE FUEL ADJUSTMENT

NEAT (Millions)	Year				
	1983	1984	1985	1986	1987
Actual Figures	(86,730)	175,604	259,453	47,286	263,729
Adjusted Figures	(128,119)	702	(5,956)	(229,459)	(217,249)
Difference	41,389	174,902	265,409	276,745	480,978
% Change	–48%	–100%	–102%	–585%	–182%

Similarly, earnings per share would have been dras-
tically lowered during the past five years if fuel costs had
not declined since 1982. In fact, with the exception of 1984,
Delta's earnings per share would have been negative. The

percentage shifts are the same as those that actually took place with net income after taxes.

What is startling, however, are the actual differences between actual and adjusted figures. In 1987, there was a $10.76 per share swing, or 182 percent change in earnings per share which dropped from $5.90 to a minus $4.86.

WHAT WOULD HAVE HAPPENED?

One cannot help but wonder what might have happened had the fuel prices remained high? Would Delta have merged with Western? Would the one-time favorable accounting change made in 1987 have been made sooner? With earnings so poor, wouldn't Delta have been ripe for a take-over by an unfriendly suitor or for some leveraged buy-out? Would Delta have been able to raise its fares? Perhaps the most pertinent question: Would Delta have done anything about its controllable expenses and, toward that end, have done the unheard-of by laying off part of its work force?

Obviously, the answers to these questions will never be known, but they raise issues regarding the vitality of the company—if not, indeed, the entire industry. With its high controllable costs, it is obvious that of all air carriers Delta is the most vulnerable to calamitous changes in fortunes that are external to the business.

So How Does Delta Conceal this Nagging Vulnerability?

THE ONE TIME ACCOUNTING CHANGE PLOY

For fiscal year 1987, ending June 30, 1987, Delta implemented substantial accounting changes in its aircraft depreciation methodology and pension plan funding. While these changes were perfectly legal and, indeed, in the case of the changes for depreciation, more accurate, the figures were masked in public reports of earnings which glorified record revenues. Apparently, Delta thinks that bigger is better and that the true financial implications of what happened in fiscal year 1987 should be conveniently ignored insofar as the public is concerned.

Delta has effectively masked the company's erratic operating income for the past eight years by the sale of its principal assets—aircraft. The fact that this strategy has been eminently successful is reflected in the fact that Delta ironically remains a darling of the investment community, a community which has never seemed to notice this change in accounting procedures.

The major changes in Delta's accounting activities were to extend the period of depreciation of aircraft owned from ten to 15 years and to make substantial changes in the employees' benefit plans.

First, Delta implemented a new accounting standard for expensing salaries and related expenses. According to the 1987 annual report to shareholders, this action resulted in a pre-tax savings of $62 million.

Secondly, Delta increased the average weighted discount rate of its employees' pension plan. This lowered the present value amount of money needed to fund the annuity on an actuarial basis for the total pension plan funding.

With regard to the depreciation methodology, assuming that existing aircraft on average have not reached the end of their ten-year depreciation cycle, the depreciation accounting change will increase net earnings per share for the period of time between the date of change and where the average asset life reaches ten years. For the subsequent five years, however—years 11 through 15—net earnings per share will decrease because of this change in methodology.

As a result of the accounting changes, Delta's figures from its 1987 annual report show an increase in net income per share from $1.18 in 1986 (an 81 percent decrease from 1985) to $5.90 per share in 1987, for a growth rate of 400 percent in net income. Operating income, which is a better index of the company's performance, was shown to have increased from .86 per share in 1986 (an 81 percent decrease from 1985) to $9.05 during the same period—for a phenomenal 952.3 percent growth in one year.

It is particularly interesting to note that instead of its reported earnings of $9.05 per share for fiscal 1987, which the company reported with great hyperbole but without explanation in its fiscal 1987 year end press release, the restated earnings of Delta turn out to be a mere $4.75 per share. This is only slightly better than its income per share in 1981 and worse than in 1984 and 1985. In other words, if Delta's fiscal 1987 earnings are calculated consistently with prior years, fiscal 1987 was in truth, a relatively poor year for Delta and certainly no record by any fair stretch.

So Where are the Vaunted Analysts of Wall Street?

The following recapitulation of analysts' reports on Delta's fiscal third quarter 1988 earnings shows how Wall Street gets carried away with revenues in the airline industry, resulting in a false euphoria.

"It was a gangbuster quarter," crowed Timothy Pettee, an analyst with Bear Stearns and Co., Inc., following Delta's 1988 fiscal second quarter ended December 31, 1987. "The numbers came in way, way above the street expectations." The *Wall Street Journal* further noted that Delta "... surprised Wall Street with a stronger than expected performance in its second quarter ...."[15]

If Mr. Pettee thinks that a quarter in which a company's profits fall 30 percent qualifies for the sobriquet "gangbuster," one has to ask what the next level of success above "gangbuster" might be.

The truth is, Delta was in its mode of selling aircraft in *both* quarters, and if Mr. Pettee had obtained a true reading of the operating income *on a constantly stated accounting basis*, he might have seen that Delta's profit of $1.82 per share was essentially even with the previous year's second quarter, notwithstanding a quarterly 42 percent rise in revenues. Delta's earning capacity seems to be marking time a full year after the Western merger.

The chart on the following page illustrates the inconsistent performance of Delta's operating and net income results on an earnings per share basis during the decade of the 1980s. Note the adjusted figures for 1987 and 1988 to eliminate the effect of accounting changes.

There were many ways in which the analysts worked over time to be enthusiastic about Delta. Some commented that while Delta's year-to-year comparisons of earnings per share were flat, the performance was exceptional because fuel costs were "significantly higher this year."[16] At the time, Delta's own director of financial planning came up with the explanation that the company was doing a better job with controlling the number of discount seats available.[17]

Fuel expenses have been the knife at Delta's throat for ten years, yet Delta's management continues to mark time. Nearly ten years ago, *The New York Times* published Delta's fourth quarter 1979 earnings, which dropped to $21.1 million, or $1.06 per share, from $34.1 million, or $1.71 a share, in the same period of 1978. Revenues increased in the same period by 23 percent to $703.8 million, compared with $574.2 million a year earlier. As *The Times* financial writer put it, "Delta blamed rising fuel costs for the profit slumps. The company's revenues per passenger mile rose 21 percent in the quarter to 10.6 cents, but that was not enough to offset the higher cost of fuel and lower capacity utilization."[18]

HOW LONG CAN THIS KIND OF THING GO ON? APPARENTLY FOREVER.

Delta's 1988 fiscal year earnings for the twelve months ended June 30, 1988 were heralded by such headlines as "Quarterly Profits Up 76% at Delta."[19] Generally, Wall Street was complimentary in its comments about Delta's earnings performance. This was true even though an unusual number of writers identified significant windfalls Delta received particularly because of the troubles at Eastern, its primary competitor.

The financial press does not earn high marks for its insightfulness because it has never taken into consideration, with any consistency, the one-time 1987 accounting change which has warped financial performances heavily in Delta's favor since fiscal year-end 1987. Delta downplays this little event at every chance. Take, for example, a chart furnished

CHANGE IN OPERATING INCOME PER SHARE
AND NET INCOME PER SHARE
THROUGHOUT THE 1980'S

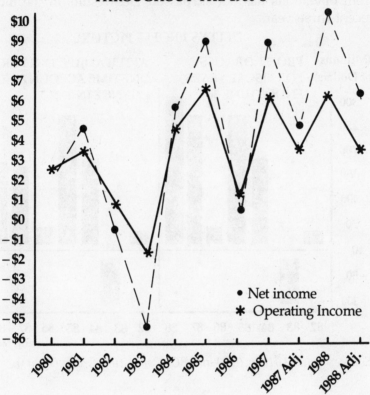

Source: BCI Consulting Group.

by Delta to the press which shows the company's profit-and-loss picture, beginning with fiscal year 1982, for the succeeding seven fiscal years ending June 30, 1988. While there are certain footnotes to that chart, what is conveniently forgotten is the one-time accounting change, implemented by Delta to mask mediocre financial performance. On the following page, that chart is reproduced on the left; on the right is the same chart adjusted in 1987 and 1988 to eliminate the effect of accounting changes allowing one to see actual profit from operations. As the figure shows, profit from operations has not surpassed 1985 results in the most recent three years.

DELTA'S PROFIT PICTURE

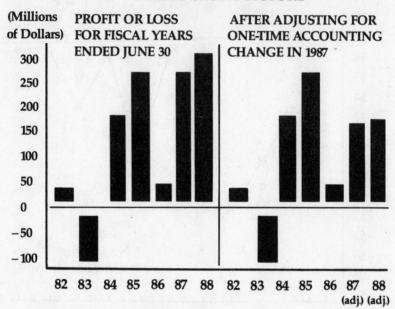

Source: Delta Airlines (left) and BCI Consulting Group (right).

If, in fact, the one-time accounting change had not been made in 1987, the following summarizes what would have happened to Delta's reported 1988 earnings:
   • Net earnings before taxes would have been 46 percent lower;
   • Net earnings after taxes and earnings per share would have been 40 percent lower;
   • Profitability ratios that measure operating and net profits would have been significantly less;
   • Operating profit would have plummeted from 7.19 percent to 4.41 percent and the net profit margins would have fallen from 4.44 percent to 2.66 percent;

• Earnings per share would have grown only 3 percent from 1987 to 1988 as opposed to the 7 percent growth
rate reported by Delta; and

• Earnings per share for 1988 would have actually
declined from $6.30 to $3.78, making 1988 only the third-
best year in the decade after 1984 and 1985.

Considering that Delta's financial reports have
included Western as a part of its system since December 18,
1986, it is not unfair to conclude that the impact of the
merger, after two full years of operation, has been neutral at
best and, probably, less than beneficial because of the
increase in expenses by 15 percent from 1987 to 1988. For
example, the average cost to fly a seat now in Delta's system
rose from 7.79 cents for the fourth quarter of 1988 from 6.94
cents in the same period in fiscal year 1987. It is disturbing
to note that salaries and benefits increased 14 percent to
$700.5 million, and this was a figure which does *not* include
a 3 to 5 percent pay increase which would not be reflected in
fiscal 1988 earnings.

On a calendar year basis, 1988 may well prove to be a
better year for the airline industry than 1984, the best year to
date since deregulation. It is difficult, therefore, if indeed
not impossible, to conceive of a better set of circumstances
currently operating in Delta's favor: extremely strong traffic
throughout 1988, particularly in the southeastern United
States, and the unprecedented problems that Eastern Airlines experiences as its assets are cannibalized and its potential is shrunk on a daily basis by the Frank Lorenzo-led
management team. In light of these advantages for Delta in
the past year, the previous chart is even more disturbing.
The extent of the effect of the accounting changes on operating and net income results reported on a per share basis is
highlighted with 1988 results on the following page.

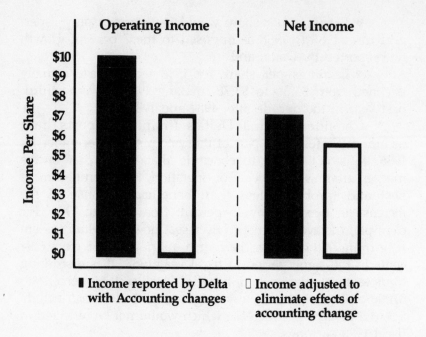

Source: *BCI Consulting Group.*

Change in 1988 operating and net income per share after adjusting
for the effects of one-time accounting changes in 1987

In that context, after thoughtful consideration, it is difficult to get excited about the quality of Delta's earnings. It becomes much easier to predict with some degree of confidence that when the economic downturn comes, as it surely will if history is any guide, Delta may well find that its cost structure will not permit it to implement changes which can prevent calamitous financial results.

Fiscal 1988's fuel expense at Delta was approximately $865 million. If 1982 fuel cost as a percent of revenues had been maintained, that figure would have been slightly over $2 billion. Such a result would have caused net earnings before taxes to drop 286 percent for a loss of $778,000,464. Net earnings and earnings per share would have plummeted 250 percent below reported earnings creating a loss of $9.42 per share.

As we have already observed, the one-time accounting changes to extend depreciation and reduce employee pension plan contributions were perfectly legal, but I have to be cynical about the timing of the change in fiscal 1987. I submit that it was Oppenlander's swan song and was undertaken in order to mask the really unexceptional results he had obtained even though Delta had become a major cash-generating operation since the Western merger. As we have seen repeatedly in this industry, revenues are one thing, but profit performance continues to be quite another.

An in-depth analysis of Delta's numbers reveal some disturbing facts:

● Controllable costs continue to climb without abatement;

● Profit performance in this decade has been unpredictable and erratic; and

● Synergisms from the Western merger, if any, are not being realized on the profit-and-loss statement two years after the merger.

Help Wanted: No PR Flacks Need Apply

The harsh conclusion that must be reached is that Delta has not been under strong financial stewardship during this decade. Its management has both ignored and willfully failed to take advantage of the dramatic and volatile economic whirlwinds at play in the airline industry since deregulation.

More than happy talk from over-optimistic analysts and drum beating from Delta's publicists will be needed to pull Delta's fat from the fire. It is time for analysts and investors to start giving Delta's management the marks it deserves. Perhaps with that kind of external pressure for change, Delta might develop the courage to set its house in order.

--------- Chapter Six ---------

The-Back-of-the-Envelope-Gang

"I don't think the [company] has
a head: its neck has just grown
up and haired over."
—John L. Lewis

Delta's Lack of a Budget Process

In its 1987 annual report to shareholders, Delta's Messrs. Garrett and Allen expounded at some length on Delta's long-range strategy.[1] In truth, Delta is not known for its strategic plans, and never has been. The most telling evidence to be mounted in defense of this amazing assertion will be found in the equally amazing fact that *the company does not have a budget process!*[2]

A company lacking an annual budget process can not begin to be effective in either making or implementing a long-range plan, let alone projecting strategic decisions, or for that matter, positioning of assets or programs for strategic advantage. That is to say without an annual budget process it is very difficult if not impossible to develop forecasts of either profit or loss and, certainly very difficult to project expenditures on either a short- or long-term basis. As any individual who has ever had administrative control of a budget process can attest, the annual budget is the basis and foundation of any form of strategic planning.

Soon after I left Delta to become general counsel of Springs Industries, Inc., a *Fortune* 500 company, one of the great shocks in my professional life was discovering that I was a key player in a budget process. It was something I had never encountered at Delta and a process for which I had no previous experience or training. My law department, which was a non-profit center of the new company, had a budget process just as tight and just as demanding as any other area of the company.

Delta, on the other hand, has a peculiar procedure which is an obvious holdover from its earliest days. In this time-honored process, every expenditure at Delta over $1,000 must be approved personally by the chief executive officer.[3] Given the nature of the airline industry, where few pieces of gear are likely to cost less than $1,000, this means that the CEO must personally approve literally thousands of such expenditures on a regular basis. In a company the size of Delta such a situation is unthinkable. It simply boggles the imagination.

It is impossible to tell whether it is ignorance or arrogance, or a combination of these, which permits Delta to cling to such an antiquated fiscal mechanism. Airlines are among the most cash-intensive businesses in the world operating in what must be one of the most volatile industrial environments imaginable. Consequently, Delta starts out with a serious handicap when external factors beyond management's control start to plague the industry. If the company does not have the forecasting tools which enable it to project trends, the results could be unexpectedly disastrous.

Delta's Missing Forecasting Ability

In addition to the absence of a budgeting process and the subsequent lack of forecasting ability, Delta suffers the additional handicap of having no formal procedure by which it can evaluate strategic alternatives or make assessments of the competition.

Further, Delta has saddled itself with an additional liability: a rigid no-layoff policy. Moreover, Delta also has no plan—or perceived plan—for permitting or encouraging early retirement of superfluous executives.

In fact, the company that has a rigid no-layoff policy is one which has lost or forfeited its ability to adapt to a constantly changing marketplace. Delta is such a company. As a result of its acquisition of Western Airlines, Delta has become bloated and overstaffed. Such a situation might be surmountable were its salary compensation not the highest in the industry. Absurdly, however, there does not seem to be either the ability—or the inclination—to address this crucial issue head-on. Should an economic recession or downturn occur, or if Delta's competition out of Atlanta should become more aggressive, this inability to lay-off employees will lay Delta low faster than anything else. Delta might then be forced to reconsider this inflexible policy on lay-offs and early retirements even earlier than Delta cares to admit.

It is difficult to comprehend the rigidity with which Delta's management functions—without a budget process and some contingency planning for work force reduction—but that is the mind set at the company today, and it is a worrisome factor for those of us who are grateful for Delta's presence in Atlanta, at least in terms of the dollars Delta generates as wages.

Actions Have Consequences Everywhere But at Delta

A case in point: An example of Delta's inability to forecast its financial performance either accurately or correctly occurred in 1981. Delta reported a 71 percent drop in profit for calendar year 1981, which it blamed on a 7 percent curtailment in operations due to the Professional Air Traffic Controllers Organization (PATCO) strike and on "uneconomic, deep-discount fares" during the summer season which it was "forced to match."[4] In the annual report to stockholders for 1981, Delta's CEO, David C.Garrett, wrote the following closing paragraph:

"In view of our expectations for the future, the Board of Directors has proposed an increase in the number of Delta's authorized shares of common stock to 100,000,000 and a 2 for 1 stock split. These proposals will be presented for stockholder approval at the annual stockholders' meeting later this year. The Board also announced its intention to increase the quarterly cash dividend by 25% if these proposals are approved."[5]

It must be concluded from the stated intention of Delta's board of directors that their "expectations for the future" were quite rosy indeed. Or else why would the company increase its quarterly payout by 25 percent and increase the authorized shares of common stock and split it, unless it had high expectations for the performance of that stock after the split? The sword of deregulation, combined with the sharp but brief recession in 1982, acted swiftly and humbled Delta accordingly.

Slightly more than a calendar year later, the following paragraph was contained in Garrett's report to stockholders for fiscal year 1983: "In recognition of the very disappointing financial results and the competitive struggles which Delta and the airline industry face over the next several years, the Board of Directors thought it prudent to reduce the dividend rate. At their regular meeting on July 28, 1983, the Board members voted to reduce the September 1983 quarterly dividend payment from $.25 to $.15 per common share."[6]

Obviously, Delta's board of directors should have been embarrassed, if indeed they were not, about the swift turn of events which caused the company to reverse its course by the reduction in the dividend pay-out, since inconsistent dividend payments are considered poor planning in business management. Clearly, their "expectations for the future" were not met. Such an embarrassing and uncomfortable surprise for an outside board of directors in most companies would have been sufficient grounds to remove, or at least demote, some of the senior officers responsible for making predictions (it is difficult to consider that it was actually a forecast). Is there no one willing to act responsibly in these boards, or do actions really have no consequences at Delta?

Dumb Luck, Not Expertise, at Delta

Another example of Delta's financial naivete occurred late in 1969 and early 1970, when Delta was negotiating for a loan of about fifty million dollars through a syndication of United Kingdom banks to finance the Rolls-Royce engines that would later be installed on the Lockheed L-1011 TriStars which the company was buying. The agent bank for the syndication was Lazard Brothers & Co., London, and the loan was cheap relative to available sources in the United States, because it was guaranteed by the Export Credit Guarantee Department of the Exchequer to stimulate exports from the United Kingdom.

During the course of negotiations of that loan, Lazard offered Delta a choice of repaying at a fixed interest rate of 6.5 percent or, alternatively, repaying at a variable rate pegged to the U.S. prime interest rate. The prime rate in the United States was then relatively low, but that would change radically in the next several years. In any case, there was no 6.5 percent money around anywhere at the time, and to opt for the latter was to assume that we would have seen a prime rate in the United States below 6.5 percent sometime soon—which was, inherently, ludicrous.

Nevertheless, Olin Galloway, then chief financial officer Oppenlander's number-two man, argued strongly for the floating rate. His premise was obviously based on a belief that longer-term interest rates would be lower than 6.5 percent. I argued strongly for the 6.5 percent rate and was supported by others in the non-financial areas of the company, including Julian May of the engineering department. Oppenlander eventually opted for the fixed rate, and would later tell an analyst who was marveling at the fact that Delta had saved so much money by fixing that rate early on (prime was close to 18 percent at the time, and the Lazard loan was not yet fully repaid), "It was just dumb luck."

Delta's Inability to Plan its International Routes

Regardless of the internal processes which Delta uses to undertake its long-range planning, its reputation for careful management and strategic planning seems nonexistent, particularly as such reputation (or lack of same) relates to international route development.

A senior officer of an aerospace company put it this way: "They [Delta] are the last of the 'back-of-the envelope guys' when it comes to strategic planning in the international arena. What I mean is that one of their senior management types is flying somewhere, gets an idea about what the company should do next month or next year, writes it down on the back of an envelope, presents it to the senior management team at its Monday morning meeting and, if a majority carries the day or if Ron Allen likes it, it becomes a strategy—regardless of whether it fits in with anything that the company has done in the past. I don't understand their international strategy, but I don't think they do either."

It is difficult to discern what Delta's plans are for its international operations. For lack of a better term, perhaps, the only way I can describe Delta's international operations is as a "crazy-quilt patchwork." A crazy-quilt patchwork is a kind of quilt made by stitching together irregularly shaped pieces of fabric in a completely random fashion. Apt enough for Delta.

It is easy enough to understand the logic behind an international system that includes such routes as Atlanta/London, Atlanta/Paris, Atlanta/Frankfurt and Atlanta/Tokyo. But what are we to make of the rest of the system—Atlanta/Shannon, Orlando/London, Cincinnati/London, Orlando/Frankfurt?

Thinking I must be missing something, some strategically justifiable reason for such routes, I happened to ask a Delta B-767 captain for his opinion. I said, "How would you describe Delta's international strategy if you were given 30 seconds to think up a phrase?"

Almost without hesitation, the captain replied, "A crazy-quilt patchwork system." I was amazed at the response, but those were exactly his words.

Delta's strategy seems to be one of a willy-nilly global expansion without a lot of logic associated with it. Traffic from Atlanta to Shannon, Ireland would probably not fill half of a B-747, so that perhaps the L-1011 is the correct choice for that route. But as strategic planning develops for these routes, the real questions become: What is driving the selection of destinations? Is it driven by a desire to position the company to garner traffic potential in cities across

Europe and Asia, or is it driven by the Delta marketing department's foolish attempt to select exotic-sounding destinations that look good on charts and posters depicting Delta's international character as an airline? I don't know the answers to these questions, and I don't think the management of the company does, either.

Planning for the Delta Fleet of the Next Century

BEEBE'S B-747 ERROR

A particularly troublesome example of Delta's lack of strategic planning is shown by its long-range plan for fleet acquisition. In May 1967, Dick Maurer, then general counsel, and I launched negotiations for the purchase of five Boeing B-747s. As usual, Delta was not the first in line to purchase the enormously popular B-747, in fact, we were about twentieth on the list. It was an important set of negotiations, however, because it was the first time that Delta had ever purchased aircraft manufactured by The Boeing Company.

Maurer and I traveled with Don Hetterman, who was director of technical operations, and were met in Seattle by John Nycum, who had long been Delta's assistant vice president for West Coast operations. After four exhilarating days in Seattle, we concluded a contract for a $100 million purchase of five Boeing B-747s. The base price of each jumbo jet was nearly $19 million, and by the time the Delta specifications were added, unit cost came closer to $22 million.

The first B-747s were delivered about two years later and were operated initially by Delta on such routes as Chicago/Miami, and Atlanta/Los Angeles. The aircraft provided a valuable competitive edge for Delta because at that time B-747s were being operated domestically on a wide scale by most of the trunk carriers in the United States. In scheduled operations today, this is no longer true, but at the time, there was competitive advantage in having the aircraft in the fleet.

In 1975, when the decision to sell the B-747s was made, the news never leaked outside of Tom Beebe's office.

When Beebe announced this fact later that year to his board of directors, no debate was permitted. *They were too big for the system. The decision had been made, period. They had to go.* If the truth were ever told, I suspect that the simple fact that Charlie Dolson, Beebe's predecessor, had bought the airplanes was probably good enough reason, in and of itself, for Beebe to get rid of them.

Eventually, three B-747s were traded back to The Boeing Company at an average price of $15 million. Boeing subsequently turned around and sold the aircraft for the same amount to Flying Tigers and less than three years later those same airplanes were each worth $28.5 million in the market-place. Delta had book losses on each of the B-747s that it sold.

Less than a calendar quarter after the last B-747 was turned back to The Boeing Company, Delta started service to London, a route for which it had an application pending well before Beebe's unilateral decision to sell the B-747s was made. The award of the Atlanta/London route was not an overnight phenomenon; application for the award had been pending for more than a year, and the executives of Delta had been lobbying President Carter endlessly for the route authority. Such a small matter did not deter Beebe, however. Three months before Delta was authorized to begin service, he sold the only airplanes the company owned or had in its stable that could operate from Atlanta to London nonstop.

Since it no longer had any long-range airplanes on hand to inaugurate service to London, Delta was forced to lease intermediate range L-1011-200 series aircraft from Trans-World Airlines. Not only did those leases come very dear to Delta, but also leasing somebody else's airplanes does not build assets on a balance sheet. Beebe had sold valuable assets at the very time they were strategically important to Delta's new Atlanta/London service, only to be forced into expensive stopgap measures to overcome this critical failure of long-range planning.

Planning for the Delta Fleet of the Next Century

THE TRISTAR WARS

In sharp contrast to Delta's handling of the B-747s is its treatment of its Lockheed L-1011 TriStars. Two years after Delta purchased the B-747 aircraft, I was once again selected by Maurer to go to Burbank, California as part of the negotiation team which was to purchase Delta's wide-bodied Lockheed L-1011 TriStar fleet. The occasion was another first for Delta because, this time, the company was a launch customer of the L-1011. Delta was one of three original customers, along with TWA and Eastern, that enabled Lockheed to commit to the aircraft's production. This position gave the company tremendous leverage in negotiating a tight package, both contractually and technically in Delta's favor.

Dolson's savvy in such negotiations was demonstrated by his adamant opposition to the installation of Rolls Royce engines on the L-1011 aircraft. Dolson felt strongly that the Rolls Royce RB-211 engine, which at the time existed only on the drawing board, should not be used on the TriStars when the already extant Pratt & Whitney engine, with its high marks in reliability, maintainability and performance, was available. In Dolson's view buying a British engine could produce enormous logistical nightmares if even the mildest of technical difficulties arose. Despite Dolson's objections, Eastern and TWA weighed in on the side of the Rolls Royce engine, thereby enabling Lockheed to put the RB-211 on all three airlines' TriStars. Dolson began to look like a prophet when Rolls Royce Aero Engines Limited, the engine manufacturer of the TriStar power plant, went into bankruptcy in 1970. This event contributed to the near-bankruptcy of Lockheed and led to a most troublesome period for purchasers of TriStars. Ultimately, Lockheed was able to stay in business only because the government of the United Kingdom nationalized Aero Engines and the U.S. Congress provided Lockheed with a guaranteed bank loan.

Delta later placed an order for additional Lockheed TriStar L-1011-500 series aircraft for its London operation, which would soon be expanded into other European cities.

Today, the long-range-series L-1011 is Delta's only long-range airplane. While the L-1011 is a fine aircraft, it represents 20-year-old aircraft technology and is a design Lockheed has not manufactured in over six years.

MISJUDGING JAPAN AIR LINES

Any serious strategic planning requires an astute intelligence-gathering mechanism which keeps the competition under a weather eye. So when Japan Air Lines signed a contract to buy five Boeing B-747-400 series aircraft, the intelligence that they would most likely be headed for JAL's new Atlanta/Tokyo nonstop service should have been old news for Delta. Confirmation of this intelligence was available recently from an internal Japan Air Lines newsletter, which announced that one of the new planes will be dedicated to the Atlanta/Tokyo route, which now covers 6,958 miles. The Boeing B-747-400 has a two man cockpit and will be able to fly 8,000 miles nonstop with a full payload of passengers and freight—the first commercial aircraft capable of doing so.

The year 1990 is probably the earliest that the nonstop service to Atlanta will start, but in the meantime, Japan Air Lines has increased the frequency of Atlanta/Tokyo flights operated through Seattle from two flights a week to three and has indicated it may well go to five by the end of 1988.

Gearing up to meet the challenge are the short-sighted long-range strategic planners at Delta. In April of 1988, Delta announced that it had purchased four more L-1011-500 TriStars from United Airlines. United, in turn, had purchased them from Pan American, which has the reputation within the industry as the most notorious abusers of airliners. Curiously, Delta thereby announced that it would meet the JAL challenge with its trusty fleet of aging L-1011-500 TriStars.

Although the L-1011 is a good plane, it only has three engines to the Boeing's four. And Delta remains loyal to its aging fleet of L-1011s notwithstanding that most knowledgeable experts in the industry are aware of the fact that Delta leaves approximately 15,000 pounds of cargo on the loading platform at Atlanta every day when its L-1011 leaves for Tokyo. Why? Because the aircraft does not have the capacity to carry an outsized or even a full load of cargo from Atlanta to Tokyo.

Delta is very proud of its publicity coup of being the airline-elect of Disney World and Disneyland. But Delta must not have been very proud when it could not help Disney officials transport building materials for the new Disney theme park in Japan because its aging and inadequate L-1011s could not carry such a heavy outsize load. Disney was forced to charter planes from a competitor to carry the materials to Japan.

THE MIND SET FOR DISASTER

So what, we might well ask, is the secret behind this persistent Delta devotion to the L-1011-500? Why didn't Delta just own up to past mistakes and buy the B-747-400 or some version of it, two years ago when it started its Tokyo service so that it could operate comfortably from the start with full passenger and cargo loads to the Orient?

"Too darned expensive," the affable Don Hetterman, currently Delta's senior vice president of technical operations, told me at dinner one night in November of 1986, shortly before Delta began operating its Atlanta/Tokyo route.

Hetterman had consistently opposed the notion of flying Delta's two-engine B-767s across the Atlantic from Atlanta to London and other cities in Europe. The same reservations apparently didn't apply to flying a three-engine aircraft almost three times as far over the Pacific. While I found the reasoning inconsistent, I was prepared to be somewhat reassured by Hetterman, who is unquestionably the finest technical expert in the airline industry today. All this would change, however, in less than two years.

A better answer came from an executive at a large aerospace firm who has been a long-time Delta observer. When asked why Delta was willing to spend millions to reconfigure its 1960s-vintage L-1011s but was not willing to spend the same money to acquire some state-of-the-art B-747s his response was both penetrating and telling. "The problem is that Delta doesn't know the difference anymore between cost and price," he said. "Delta is building a 'leg down' by deploying an airplane over the pond [the Pacific Ocean] that is 90 percent owned by B-747s. Our company's experience suggests that Asians, for whatever reasons, feel it is actually a matter of pride to ride in a B-747. As a result, 90 percent of the passenger aircraft operating over the Pacific are B-747s."

THE EXORBITANT COST OF PROCRASTINATION

Airline and aerospace observers were expecting, indeed predicting, that Delta would announce the purchase of new long-range aircraft at its July 1988 board meeting. In fact, the speculation was that the company would place an order for the McDonnell-Douglas MD-11, a variant of the highly successful DC-10 with extended long-range and cargo-carrying capacity, for the Boeing B-747-400, or, perhaps the Airbus Industrie A-340 four-engine aircraft which are just beginning to be built in Toulouse, France. Speculation was intense because it is well known that Delta desperately needed to do something to replace its aging L-1011s. Most speculators were predicting that Delta would purchase a few B-747-400s and a few MD-11s, or maybe one or the other exclusively.

When the fateful day came, the company's famed long-range planners postponed Delta's decision with the promise to "look at it again before the end of the year."

Postponement—let's call it by its right name, "procrastination"—in the purchase of needed aircraft is a very expensive decision. Why? The facts of aircraft production schedules speak for themselves. The longer the purchase decision is delayed, the further delivery positions are extended. Even a preferred customer like Delta may have difficulty buying B-747-400s and receiving delivery before the end of 1994, a full four years after Japan Air Lines will have placed its B-747-400s in service. Moreover, in its delay-bound wisdom, Delta would pay in 1988 dollars somewhere between 8 and 12 percent more for an airplane which has a base price of $120 million.

As recently as September 1988, Delta's CEO, Ron Allen, was weighing, for the first time in his career, a decision which would have a material impact on Delta's survivability. Allen had to decide soon what airplane or what combination of airplanes would provide Delta's long-range lift well into the next century. Given his lack of knowledge about aircraft, their performance specifications and the features new aircraft might hold in common with the balance of the Delta fleet, Allen was no doubt being pounded daily by different constituencies within Delta which wanted different aircraft for different reasons. In its traditionally conservative way, the marketing department argued for the MD-11, which is less expensive and carries fewer passengers than the B-747-400, while the technical operations people no doubt advised that the B-747-400 is the aircraft the company needs from an operational point of view to continue Delta's expansion into the international market. Delta was incapable of making the right decision in these deliberations, and, I thought, would no doubt shoot itself in the wing once more.

All of this was confirmed on September 22, 1988, when Delta announced it was placing the largest airliner order in the history of the industry—for as many as 215 aircraft, to be manufactured by both McDonnell-Douglas and The Boeing Company and valued at as much as $10.5 billion.[7]

As predicted, Delta selected the MD-11, manufactured by McDonnell-Douglas, to be its long-range aircraft for service to the Orient. Thus Delta casts in concrete its "leg down" over the Pacific. No MD-11s have yet been built, let alone flown, and question marks still remain about the viability of the MD-11 program, although there is no gainsaying that the Delta order gave the MD-11 program a tremendous boost.

More important, though, Delta has chosen to compete with the progeny of an airplane that was never intended to compete head on with the B-747. So, it seems, Beebe's ghost still haunts Delta.

"They're still afraid of the big airplane," a senior aerospace official told me by telephone on the day after the announcement of Delta's order was made, adding, "Either that, or they won't own up to Beebe's mistake of selling the original 747s."

Interestingly enough, the Delta order included nine extended-range two-engine Boeing B-767s which Delta intends to operate on " ... its flights to Europe."[8]

TWA, American and Piedmont have each been flying B-767s to Europe for a few years now, at an estimated savings in fuel costs of more than $10,000 per flight. Two years hence, Delta will be able to compete effectively, at least on an efficiency basis, some five years after the fact.

Inability to Take Blame for Failure

Pointing to external factors beyond its control is a favored way at Delta of shifting the blame away from its poor management. Portraying itself as helpless before the fluctuating fortunes of the industry has been a standard technique at Delta throughout this decade. By such corporate wringing of hands, the company is tacitly admitting that it merely reacts to external forces at play in the industry and that it lacks any ability to be proactive in defense of its own fate. So long as Delta refuses to develop a strategy to cope effectively with such problems as deep discount fares and with increases in uncontrollable costs, such as fuel prices, it will continue to drift toward disaster.

More to the point, so long as Delta continues to neglect the basic tools of strategic planning—a proscribed budget process, reliable mechanisms of fiscal forecasting, competitive industry intelligence—it will remain its own worst enemy.

It is obvious however, that responsibility for this adverse predicament cannot be ascribed solely to Delta's senior management, but must be shared by its external board of directors. They have not only refused to require that actions have consequences but have also failed to demand that fiduciary responsibilities be taken seriously by the institution of a thorough-going budgetary reform.

Chapter Seven

The Delta Dog in Atlanta's Manger

"Prudence is a rich ugly old
maid courted by incapacity."
—William Blake

Airport and Airway Congestion: Has
Deregulation Spawned Delays?

Recent evidence suggests that the U.S. scheduled airlines now send approximately 17,000 flights into the air every day. These flights experience nearly 2,000 hours of delay on a daily basis with an annual loss of passenger time which is valued at approximately $1 billion. Moreover, this massive delay increases the annual operating cost of the airlines an estimated $2 billion.[1]

The issue of airport and airway congestion is not new to the airline industry. Schedule delays in the industry reached a peak in the 1960s when the New York, Washington and Chicago airports, commonly known as the "Golden Triangle," had to be placed under a formal process whereby landings and take-offs were regulated. Airlines were allotted "slots" at various periods when landing at the airports. Beyond that, no airline could take off or land without prior approval. While this was relatively easy to manage before deregulation, after deregulation managing airport entry and exit and limiting or controlling airway space became critical issues nearly impossible to resolve.

How is it that airline delays have now become more prominent than in any other period under nine years of deregulation?

BENIGN NEGLECT IS TO BLAME

One answer is that in 1979, the first year of deregulation, the U.S. airline industry had nearly 5.5 million annual departures and did not reach that level again until 1984. Rising fuel costs, a major U.S. economic recession and the air controller's strike of the early '80s held down scheduled operations. From this point of view, this slowdown all brought about a period of benign neglect in the system, one perhaps similar to the current worldwide relaxation on the demand for energy-efficient machinery as crude oil prices continue to decline. As more aircraft and aircraft departures move into the system and as the increasing use of airport hubs expands the pressure on the physical infrastructure of the airline industry, the delay factor becomes more severe.

A HUGE INCREASE IN PASSENGER VOLUME IS TO BLAME

In 1987, it was estimated that aircraft departures had exceeded those logged in 1984 by some 26 percent. The dramatic airline growth experienced during this period reflects an increase in passengers using air transportation: an estimated 344 million people actually boarded aircraft in 1984, while more than 450 million passengers used the same services in 1987. The delays the industry experiences, this argument would have us believe, are caused by these additional 100 million passengers clamoring for access to the same facilities which had earlier handled its departures in a timely fashion.

THE REAGAN ADMINISTRATION IS TO BLAME

Increased air traffic is not the only culprit involved in creating the endemic passenger delay at airports. Critics of the Reagan administration assert that the executive branch has failed to play its part in the critical area of air traffic control, pointing out that there are still about 25 percent fewer controllers than before the PATCO strike. According to the Senate Commerce Committee, that is at least 1,000 fewer than there should be.

Critics point to the Reagan Administration's lack of effective action to correct the imbalance in the population of air traffic controllers occasioned by Reagan's handling of the PATCO strike. In addition, they observe that the root causes of the PATCO strike still exist, and the woefully inadequate air traffic control systems have not been sufficiently modernized to handle the increased burden of traffic. These concomitant delays have brought considerable pressure on Congress to re-impose some form of regulation on the airlines, seen by some as the only solution to the administration's bungling.[2] This pressure has not been moderated by the publicity surrounding the rise in the number of near collisions between aircraft. According to the National Transportation Safety Board, the number of near-collisions increased by nearly 30 percent during the first seven months of 1987, compared with the same period in 1986. The total for 1986 was reported to be 839, up by 9.5 percent from 1985.

And the problem is not that there is no money to deal with these issues. Indeed a Federal Aviation Trust Fund receives $8 of every $100 paid by passengers for air transportation. This trust fund was created to generate enough financial muscle to guard against airport and airway congestion and to improve safety. How has this fund been used since Reagan took office? Instead of utilizing this fund as it was intended, the Reagan administration has refused to spend $5 billion of that trust fund so that the federal budget deficit will appear smaller than it really is.

LACK OF SECONDARY AIRPORTS IS TO BLAME

One effective way to moderate delays is the increased use of older airports, a solution that is actually being applied more often than is generally recognized. For example, Chicago's Midway Airport, once used only by Midway Airlines, has gained additional tenants. Both United and Continental propose to use this airport in addition to the main Chicago airport, O'Hare. Airlines have also provided increased service at White Plains, New York, for business executives who would otherwise have to use New York's LaGuardia or John

F. Kennedy Airports. Despite considerable political crossfire, Love Field, in Dallas, also appears to be opening up to more carriers. So, this argument goes, the failure of airlines to identify these secondary airports as a short-term solution and to move into them with some dispatch indicates that the delays are not necessarily a problem of too few landing strips and too many flights, but rather a problem of the creative utilization of existing facilities.

In Atlanta, Delta is to Blame

Read on, then, about the issue of a secondary airport in Atlanta, and the position taken by Delta, which perennially has had one of the worst on-time performances in the industry, according to the reports it files with the Department of Transportation.

Consider, too, that in 1987, Hartsfield Atlanta was second only to Boston's Logan Airport in the top five airports in the country with most delays per 1000 operations.

At the end of 1987, Hartsfield Atlanta succeeded Chicago's O'Hare as the world's busiest airport, with 801,122 operations versus O'Hare's 795,804 operations.[3] This was the first time that Atlanta had outstripped Chicago in this statistical distinction, and while the news may have been an occasion for Atlanta's publicists to celebrate, it only increased the chagrin of Atlanta's airline travelers, for whom it only confirmed what they already knew.

Since it opened in 1980, Hartsfield's traffic has increased about 30 percent. While the growth appears to be reaching a mature rate there still may be cause for concern. John Braden, director of marketing and public relations for Hartsfield Atlanta International Airport, points out that the airport was designed to handle 750,000 flights per annum. But, as Braden notes, this is a theoretical figure and assumes no delay per flight. To the extent that an airline is willing to accept delays, then it can increase its capacity accordingly. For example, for 1988 it is estimated that there will be approximately 800,000 flights in and out of Hartsfield, which creates an average delay of four minutes per flight.

Braden says that this is acceptable, but if the number increases to, say, one million flights, the average flight delay becomes more like 20 minutes, which is unacceptable and will dramatically increase the demand for a second airport.

It should come as no surprise to the citizens of Atlanta that the airport is an essential hub of prosperity for the city of Atlanta, the state of Georgia and, indeed, the Southeast. A study commissioned by the city of Atlanta, designed to analyze Hartsfield's relationship with its sur-roundings, was released in August 1987. Conducted by two separate accounting firms, the study demonstrates that the airport pumped $6.25 billion into the local economy in 1986, with the expectation that it would generate close to $7 billion by the end of 1987.[4]

More importantly, another study conducted by the Atlanta Chamber of Commerce showed that the availability of air service at Hartsfield was one of the main reasons corporations select Atlanta over other cities as a site for offices.

According to a 1987 study for the city of Atlanta prepared by the accounting firm of Peat, Marwick & Mitchell, Hartsfield traffic should exceed 900,000 flights a year by 1990. The study also projected that Hartsfield's physical parameters could not be expanded to handle any capacity beyond that. Obviously, if Atlanta expects to con-tinue to grow, the viability of its airport facilities is of paramount importance. Just as obviously, that seems to indicate that a second airport is in Atlanta's future.

But the problems created by an overburdened Hartsfield Airport are not only Atlanta's problems. As even a casual air traveler knows, the effect of delays at Hartsfield can have domino effects on every major city in the United States. This fact was demonstrated quite clearly during the Thanksgiving and Christmas weekends of 1986 and 1987. In each of these busy periods when most U.S. airports were overflowing with holiday travelers, Hartsfield experienced substantial delays and cancellations because of bad weather, principally fog. Weather delays are not limited to the fall and winter periods at Hartsfield; thunderstorms during the late summer afternoons are not unusual. Often, ferocious winds, which rapidly shift direction, cause chaos at Hartsfield because runway headings must be changed in an attempt to reduce the effect of these wind reversals. This inevitably results in hundreds of delayed flights.

Hartsfield's weather-related delays create problems at other airports around the nation. It is not unusual for flights to be held at gates in cities like Washington, New York or Boston when storm problems plague Atlanta. Delays and cancellations in Atlanta affect connecting and direct flights to Europe, the Orient, and arrivals and departures from literally every major airport in the United States.

Each delay suggests that Hartsfield is coming precipitously close to the edge of saturation and its current advantages—direct flights to nearly everywhere—will become less attractive as travelers seek less troublesome alternatives, such as American's new hubs at Nashville and Raleigh-Durham.

A second airport for Atlanta seems therefore to be an urgent agenda item if Atlanta wishes to retain its image of the capital city of the Southeastern United States. Yet Atlanta is one of the last remaining large cities in America which has not either developed secondary satellite airport facilities to accommodate its local demand and encourage continued growth or, alternatively, developed a firm plan for building a new, replacement airport. For good reason.

It turns out that the problem of an overloaded Hartsfield and the delays it causes through the nation's flight lines is not merely one of increased passenger flow, or one of benign neglect or even the result of Reagan's budget deficits. It is a problem compounded enormously by Delta's stranglehold on the Hartsfield facility.

The simple fact is that no competitive airline can penetrate Hartsfield because the present leaseholds there— all the ticket counters, gate areas, loading facilities, baggage sorting and delivery facilities—were "grandfathered" relatively cheaply to both Delta and Eastern as original signatories for the construction of the existing concourses at

Hartsfield. This monopolistic hold on ground services is at the discretion of both Delta and Eastern, which have absolutely no business incentive to accommodate a new competitive entrant to the gridlocked Atlanta market. Over the near term, no relief is in sight because of the steadfast dominance at Hartsfield by Delta and Eastern, who collectively account for almost 90 percent of the airport's total passenger enplanements.

Both Eastern and Delta in the past have "offered" one or more gates to potential new entrants. The asking "all services price," i.e., a premium paid to the sublessor, Delta or Eastern, for servicing a new, competitive entrant, has proved prohibitive because prospective entrants cannot afford the tariff.

In short, while paying lip service to the notion that they would, for a price, allow new carriers to come into Atlanta, both Delta and Eastern have set that price high to lock the gates. Consequently, in addition to the problem of simple overloading of Hartsfield's facilities, we must add the special interests of Delta and Eastern, for whom a second airport would mean the probable loss of their virtual monopoly on the lucrative Atlanta market.

And this market is certainly lucrative! The respected British publication, *Euromoney*, estimates that the average passenger flying to and from Atlanta, Delta's principal hub, pays an average of $.22 per mile, whereas the average fare on all other Delta routes, such as Dallas/New York, where American competes head-on, is only $.13 per mile. None of this has anything to do with the cost of using Atlanta/ Hartsfield International Airport, since through passengers, who only change planes in Atlanta, pay only $.18 per mile.[5]

So who gets squeezed most by this fare structure in and out of Atlanta? None other than the Atlanta resident, who is supposedly loved and courted by Delta. Delta should be in love with the Atlanta passenger who continues to pay these outrageous costs as a penalty for a Delta cartel in Atlanta and, at the same time, continues to hold Delta in such high esteem.

Given Delta's obvious self-interest in maintaining the status quo and, as a major player in the region's economy, its equally obvious ability to shape municipal decisions, certain things begin to become increasingly clear. For example, if Atlanta should elect to build a second major airport, current estimates are that it would take a minimum of ten years to complete and cost between $2 billion and $10 billion. Yet so far as I can determine, the wheels have not even begun to be put in motion for such a project in the Atlanta area.

Even if Atlanta were to build such a major airport to replace Hartsfield—as Denver has recently done in its decision to replace Stapleton Airport for example—the time constraints involved are such that planners and airlines alike would turn inevitably to the issue of developing a second existing airport. While it is true that dual services from the same metro area would require Delta and Eastern to duplicate essential resources such as manpower and aircraft to accommodate essentially the same market areas, examples do exist of parallel services in Washington, New York, Chicago, Dallas, Houston, and Los Angeles where carriers serve both a major airport and a secondary airport with equal success.

It might be easy to understand and, perhaps, even justify, Delta's opposition to a second airport if alternative facilities did not already exist and if there were no evidence of increased local demand for a more competitive fare structure. But neither is the case in Atlanta. Notwithstanding these physical and market realities, Delta has actively discouraged the establishment of alternative facilities.

What Price Does Atlanta Pay for Delta's Opposition?

Delta's continued opposition to a secondary facility has already begun to curtail Atlanta's business growth. Here is one case in point: IRM Insurance, which had been headquartered in New York for 27 years, narrowed its field of search for a new corporate headquarters location to Atlanta, Chicago and Charlotte, North Carolina.

Chicago was eliminated early on because of its weather, but Charlotte and Atlanta remained in a dead heat as city of choice. R. Bruce Jamieson, president of IRM, finally selected Charlotte as the new headquarters of his company after reviewing all the evidence. Jamieson cited as the basis for his decision the fact that in his opinion, the City of Atlanta was geographically more fractionalized with "less harmony" in the stewardship of the city than in Charlotte.

But Jamieson cited another reason for rejecting Atlanta. He complained that Atlanta's most desirable housing is on the north side of the city, while Hartsfield Atlanta International is on the south side. Jamieson did not wish to incur the many time-consuming trips to and from potential home sites or executive office locations which the location of Hartsfield dictated. In Charlotte, Jamieson reported that the average trip from either the executive office or the homes of his executives to Charlotte Douglas International Airport is only a 20-minute drive.[6]

As if to underscore the effect these delays will have on the continued economic development of Atlanta, one FAA official, Sam Austin, remarked recently: "If we continue to put more and more traffic into Hartsfield without offering some relief, you're going to be experiencing 30-, 40-, or 60-minute delays. At that point people are going to say, 'Should I fool with Hartsfield?'"[7] That indeed may be the question which the executives of companies looking to relocate to Atlanta ask with greater frequency, "Why should I fool with Hartsfield or, for that matter, with Atlanta."

Fulton County Airport: The Alternative Delta Opposes

Fulton County Airport, affectionately known as Charlie Brown Field after the County Commissioner for whom it is unofficially named, is strategically and conveniently located only eight miles west of Atlanta's central business district. Not only is it accessible by four major interstate highway systems and two major trunk line railroad systems, but it is also closer to Atlanta's fast-growing North side community than Hartsfield. Indeed, it is clear that Fulton County Airport, an existing facility with extended runways and precision landing facilities, needs only construction of jetways to make it a viable commercial airport. Moreover, situated as it is in the northwest quadrant of the city, it is not only adjacent to neighborhoods where the city's most affluent and thus most frequent air travelers reside, it is also approximately two miles closer to the critical downtown business district of Atlanta than is Hartsfield, ten miles south of downtown. Consequently, Fulton County Airport adds convenience of access to its other attractive qualities.

But Fulton County Airport has advantages other than proximity to prime residential and corporate locations. It is also located adjacent to the 1,800-acre Fulton Industrial Area, the largest warehouse distribution center east of the Mississippi River. In addition, the Fulton Industrial Area is anchored by both the 240-acre Atlanta Industrial Park and the 250-acre Westpark Industrial Park.

At present, the Fulton County Airport serves only general aviation interests and houses the corporate fleets of Atlanta's largest and most successful and influential business names such as the Coca-Cola Company, Cox Broadcasting, Georgia-Pacific and, more recently, the R.J. Reynolds Company. These corporate users enjoy the obvious benefits of close-in proximity to downtown and the North side, where the majority of their executives live. They also enjoy uncongested air traffic control, since Fulton County's climb and descent quadrants are distinctly separate and protected from Hartsfield's.

The strategic and economic benefits of Fulton County Airport are no secret to the commercial airlines. In fact, active and aggressive solicitation to open the facilities to commercial flights has been long-standing and continuous—but to no avail, thanks in large part to Delta's effective opposition.

Public debate on the issue of converting Fulton County Airport to a satellite for Hartsfield surfaced more than five years ago, as Atlanta's aviation planners identified a "consensus" for future relief of Hartsfield's needs. The Atlanta Regional Commission, together with a Fulton County staff study and an APADA master plan update, all pointed to Fulton County Airport as the best-suited, near-term airport satellite for Hartsfield's rapidly escalating saturation.

At about the same time, several start-up airlines, creatures of deregulation, began to inquire about the Atlanta community's interest and the economic feasibility of opening a second— clearly *secondary*—airport in Atlanta. It was during these initial cursory reviews that Delta's opposition became quietly active and instrumental in discouraging the airport's conversion.

Recognizing Delta's prominent hometown posture as a large, profitable and growing employer, it was apparent from the outset that a Delta assistant vice president had drafted a resolution which the Fulton County Commissioners employed in 1983 to restrict use of Brown Field to general aviation only. The resolution was quickly seconded by one of the commissioners, who coincidentally is currently employed by Delta.

After considerable dialogue among the Commission and both the Federal Aviation Administration and the Department of Transportation had transpired, the Department of Municipalities informed the Commission of its potential legal liabilities for restraining use of the facility designated for and receiving public use federal funding. With great reluctance the Commission reluctantly tabled the Delta assistant vice president's resolution and subsequently replaced it with a more general statement of "intents and purpose."

Since that early inquiry by outside interests, repeated attempts have been advanced to seek commercial airline service at Fulton County Airport. Most recently, Southwest Airlines, of Dallas, has offered to put $8 million in front-end money in escrow for the construction of jetway facilities at Fulton County.

To date, Delta has been persistent in its efforts to delay, if indeed not prevent, Fulton County's airfield conversion. Not content with the overt use of its own economic and political muscle to this end, Delta officials have covertly sought since 1984 to limit damage to its public image by encouraging neighborhood opposition to the potential opening of Brown Field as a satellite airport. In this way, opposition to the project is deflected from charges of obvious self-interest and made to appear to be widespread throughout the community. To this end, Delta officials meet periodically with area clergy and visit with the city newspaper editorial staff to ensure that sufficient emphasis is given to such considerations as impending noise, pollution and congestion.

Delta continues to disregard the enormous economic interests vested in the opening of a second airport. In 1985, for example, the Fulton County Commission staff calculated that the opening of the second facility would translate into 2,600 airport jobs, a local airport employee payroll of more than $16 million, and a total economic impact combining primary and induced stimulants of more than $65 million per year.

By persisting in its opposition to the creation of a secondary airport at Fulton, Delta continues to generate a considerable body of ill-will throughout the Atlanta city government, the Fulton County Commission and indeed among the people of Atlanta whom it has long named part of its "Delta family." As a consequence, Delta has now lost the "home court" advantage that it might have enjoyed had it recognized the synergism associated with opening Fulton County Airport as a second airport on terms and conditions which it undoubtedly could have dictated at the time initial discussions surfaced.

There is recent evidence that the Atlanta City Council and the Georgia Industry and Trade Commission are growing increasingly weary of Delta's dog-in-the-manger attitude. Moreover, they are justifiably weary of trying to drag the airlines into realistic discussions in how best to assist them in the selection of a second airport.

This project has been on the drawing board for nearly two decades and continues to face unrelenting opposition from Delta and its allies. The central contest in this arena is between the major economic interests which flourish or deteriorate in direct proportion to the ability of Hartsfield to service Atlanta's transportation needs efficiently and economically on the one hand, and Delta's determination to maintain its domination of Hartsfield as the only commercial airport in the Atlanta market on the other. At some point in this contest, the prestige and economic clout of Delta will buckle and the secondary airport will be built, or Delta will sustain its monopoly and Atlanta will begin to slip from its economic leadership position in the Southeast.

The balance may already have shifted, as the Atlanta City Council was told recently that the city could finance the first phase of a second major airport without any money from the airlines. Once liberated from the need to draw upon the financial support of the airline industry, it is possible that the region's government entities may find that their own economic self-interest is not the same as that of Delta.

What will eventually happen to more entrepreneurial interests remains to be seen, but it is essential to understand that this contest is yet another dramatic example of Delta's inept and reactionary managerial style which must be modified, if not abandoned, for Delta to preserve any form of leadership and customer loyalty into the twenty-first century.

Coda—The Delta Dog: A Creature of Consistent Self-Interest

It will be difficult for some to accept that Delta could be so self-serving. It is certainly not an image that Delta seeks to project in the Atlanta market. However, such questionable behavior is by no means isolated. Perhaps the most telling episode in Delta's relationship with its municipal surroundings, played the greatest role in convincing me that Delta was not a company I could long support.

In late 1978, Delta's tax department, which was under the finance department and thus ultimately reported to Bob Oppenlander, filed a protest in Clayton County, the situs of most of Delta's property and assets at the Atlanta airport. Since Delta's assets constituted over 10 percent of the tax digest, a mandatory hearing before the Clayton County Tax

Commission was triggered. As a result, the legal department was asked to help the tax department prepare for the hearing and Hunter Hughes, who had since left the legal staff and joined the Atlanta law firm of Rogers & Hardin, was engaged as outside counsel. During the course of the investigation, in which I participated actively, it became evident that historically Delta had filed inconsistent ad valorem and other property tax returns regarding the location of its assets for purposes of taxation on the tax date.

While there were no allegations of wrongdoing, a few representatives of the tax department made spurious representations that the company did everything "to cheat its best" on avoiding taxes which were properly due. After a rather thorough investigation it became a consensus among the lawyers that there were some significant irregularities in Delta's tax returns over the years. As a result the company had apparently consistently underpaid its taxes.

At the time the matter came to a head, David Garrett was in New York and Jim Callison, who had been general counsel for less than a year, went to New York to meet Garrett personally. Garrett was in New York, incidentally, to receive the B'nai B'rith Man of the Year Award. Garrett told Callison, in effect, that he was getting off on the wrong foot as the new general counsel of the company and to mind his own business. To his great credit, Callison was not cowed by that admonition and went straight to Bob Oppenlander with a request that the matter be thoroughly investigated. Oppenlander responded angrily that the tax department, in essence, was his territory and if there was an investigation to be made, he would have it done internally. He steadfastly refused to cooperate with the legal department.

I went to my former boss, Dick Maurer, then vice chairman of the board, and to my very deep regret and disappointment, Maurer responded that there was nothing he could do about the matter. That is the one and only time that I was truly disappointed in Dick Maurer.

Finally, because the lawyers persisted, I think, Arthur Andersen & Co., the company's independent auditors, were asked to "review the matter." Interestingly enough, the investigation was handled by the Arthur Andersen engagement partner for Delta who concluded that while there might have been some irregularities in the past, and that the firm might have done things differently if it had been asked to advise, there were no deficiencies or evidence of fraudulent or criminal conduct. Remember, this was Delta's "independent auditors" who were making these findings.

Traditionally, if the matter had been handled correctly, Oppenlander would have opened his heart and soul to the investigation. He would have cooperated in it and, indeed, encouraged the audit committee of the board to hire another independent accounting firm to investigate the matter. Then, if irregularities were found, he would have seen that the culprits were brought to task and that all back taxes were promptly paid—unless, of course, Opplenlander himself knew something was amiss. It was the lawyers' consensus, at least among the Delta staff, that senior management had stonewalled the whole matter.

This is a sad little story, but it persuaded me that there is a life after Delta and set the stage for my departure, not because I am a "goody two-shoes," but because of my loss of respect and disillusionment with the management of the company that until then, I thought, flew with the angels.

----------- Chapter Eight -----------

Hang Down Your Head, Tom Beebe

"Life—the way it really is—is
a battle not between Bad and
Good but between Bad and Worse."
—Joseph Brodsky

Father Delta

"A fish rots at the head first," Michael Dukakis remarked recently as he described the origins of the 1988 Pentagon Scandal. His implication was that because the Reagan team had such a poor attitude toward dedicated government service, they had provided the model which had resulted in greed and massive financial mismanagement.

Perhaps that is exactly why it is important to limn a portrait of Tom Beebe and his perspectives at Delta. Much of what I see wrong with Delta these days owes a great deal to his tenure as CEO of the company. To understand where Delta went wrong, study Tom Beebe.

Beebe the Man

Tom Beebe was a tall, lanky man with bushy eyebrows who had an odd smile hung perpetually on his long and angular face; it is said that he smiled with the bad news as well as the good. He was slightly stooped, a chain smoker, and after his serious heart problems developed his skin always had a gray pallor. Beebe appreciated fine clothes and always loved to play the country squire which included owning a string of trotting horses and maintaining a horse farm in the countryside. In fact, he had his first heart attack as he was promenading prior to a trotting race.

Beebe was not what you would call a likeable guy. He was a man governed by moods and, as I had occasion to discover, tended to be very unpredictable.

In 1969, I authored an article—written on weekends at the Emory Law School library—which I submitted in the national competition of the American Bar Association's prestigious Section of Corporation Banking and Business Law. As a young lawyer, I was elated when the letter announcing the first prize award came from the chairman of the Section. I showed it to my boss, Dick Maurer, who copied it and proudly circulated it to the senior officers of the company, who for the most part penned the typical "Congrats," or words to that effect which such awards elicit. When the copy of the letter Maurer had sent to Beebe returned, across it was scrawled: "I thought I would die laughing."

Maurer and I had a good laugh, too, although ours was of the slightly nervous variety.

That he was a peculiar man goes without saying. I have known few men who were as genuinely loathed by employees at all levels who came into contact with him at Delta. Part of his failure to win over his fellow workers was surely due to an arrogance he conveyed so persistently, that and his idiosyncratic habit of nearly always wearing an odd grin on his face, regardless of the context or of the potentially inappropriate message this projected. It was as if he were so self-satisfied with the heights of corporate power to which his machinations had brought him that the smile was a constant verification that he was top dog.

Always impeccably dressed, Beebe loved to drive exotic sports cars and to race Standardbred horses, driving the sulkies himself. To this day I remain convinced that he knew more about the horses he raised than the airline business. I remember not a few meetings when Pre Ball, then the vice president—flight operations, and a crusty veteran line pilot for Delta, would shake his head in total disbelief when Beebe made some uninformed statement or other, as, for example, the need to get rid of the five Boeing B-747s in the Delta fleet.

There can be no gainsaying that during Beebe's tenure, Delta prospered mightily; the company was an outstanding critical success in the pre-deregulation industry. Yet to what degree Beebe contributed to that success, I remain unsure. He had inherited Dolson's decentralized management team, which performed with eminent success for Delta through that period of time which led up to deregulation in 1978. The division heads knew their business, were seasoned veterans of the industry and made the most of gaining new rate and route authority under the paternalistic Civil Aeronautics Board.

To Beebe, Delta was very like those exotic cars he drove. They were created by visionary designers, crafted by gifted machinists, and tuned by seasoned mechanics. They were great cars whether he drove them or not, and so, by the same lights, was Delta a great company.

If Tom Beebe had any gift, it was as a manipulator of the system that controlled the power at Delta. He knew how to seize it and to reduce his competition to helplessness. But what new ideas did he contribute? What new systems did he build? What new structures did he create? In my opinion, he did not contribute anything to the company on a day-to-day basis, nor did he have to. It is as simple as that.

The Early Days

Beebe joined Citizens & Southern Airlines in early 1947 as director of personnel, leaving a position at United Aircraft Corporation, prior to which, during World War II, he had held an important position with Pratt & Whitney. When Delta acquired Citizens & Southern Airlines in 1953, Beebe became the head of personnel of the combined companies and brought with him a wide experience of personnel problems confronted by the industry. Not long after the acquisition was complete, union militarism appeared to be on the rise at Delta. Beebe was called on to fight the likes of Jimmy Hoffa as well as some lesser luminaries in the Air Line Pilot's Association, an organization no less strident than Hoffa's Teamsters.

To his credit, Beebe was able to stave off the unions by meeting employee demands, without "giving away the store," as the saying goes. The experience, however, must have left a deep and permanent scar for Beebe because during his tenure as chief executive, he worked tirelessly to minimize union activity at Delta. In order to keep the so-called "undesirables" from the Delta work force, Beebe frequently risked incurring the wrath of various civil rights and activists groups. For Tom Beebe, the classic undesirable was a male flight attendant.

Besides being a tireless anti-union campaigner, Tom Beebe was also a skilled organizer and politician. This talent was exercised in a fundamental way during the period of transition which took place following the death of C.E. Woolman, founder of Delta and architect of its monumental successes. Woolman had been a patriarch's patriarch—both in the worst and best senses. As patriarchs will often do, Woolman had a complete open-door policy. In this way Woolman let it be known that managers and officers were free to circumvent their superiors and come directly to him with their concerns. In short, he *was* the chain of command.

This created some serious problems. For example, when Delta acquired Citizens & Southern in 1953, at least two outstanding executives of Citizens & Southern left because of their inability to acclimate themselves to the Delta "open door" policy. They were apparently unable to function within the double bind this one-man chain of command put them in. On the one hand, they were executives with subordinates; on the other, they had the same access to the ultimate arbiter of all disputes as did everyone else. Just before Woolman died, however, this double bind had become a serious problem for the company, and senior executives, led by Beebe himself, had already started to make certain changes in the organizational structure, at least on a pro forma basis. This they did completely without telling Woolman; they had to—or the company couldn't function—was their rationale. It was a kind of palace coup in the name of efficiency.

Suddenly, after Woolman's death, there was a flourishing organizational chart. This is dramatically demonstrated by noting that before the annual shareholders meeting in 1967, there were only three assistant vice presidents of the company; after that meeting, there were 13 and, by the same time in the fall of 1969, there were 24. Beebe's reorganization team was already hard at work.

Beebe was elected to Delta's board of directors in 1967 and after C. E. Woolman's death in 1966 was named as senior vice president—personnel effective January 1967. At the same time, David Garrett was elevated to the position of senior vice president—operations. At the board meeting held following the annual meeting of shareholders in 1967, the board of directors elected a number of officers, mostly "assistants," a move which reflected Charlie Dolson's increased emphasis on decentralization of the management team. The core senior management team of senior vice presidents was left intact, however.

The Beebe/Allen Phenomenon

Shortly after his elevation, Beebe took a young analyst in the methods section of the personnel department, Ronald W. Allen, under his wing. Admired for his Nordic good looks, Allen was tall, blond, athletic, the embodiment of "cleancut" or, perhaps what we would later come to characterize as the Yuppie. Allen had come to work for Delta three years earlier, immediately after graduation from Georgia Tech, so that unlike other executives with diversified backgrounds, he had no experience in aviation, either in the military or with a competitor. He was, purely and simply, Beebe's creature, and it was something Beebe was proud of. Some of us who knew the value of solid aviation experience would later cringe when, after he had become a senior vice president and was enplaned on a Western Airlines flight to Seattle, he glibly admitted that he had never flown another airline in his entire life except Delta, until, that is, that very Western flight.

The relationship between Beebe and Allen strength-ened. In fact, he seemed like the proverbial son-in-law. Of course, that was not the case.

Behind the scenes, Beebe arranged for Allen to be named a full vice president, a phenomenon unheard of at that time in Delta's history. This event demonstrates the clout that Beebe had with his fellow officers, not to mention the external board of directors. It was no secret any longer; Allen was Beebe's protege and was on a fast track that would, eventually, stampede Allen's career interests over those of such long-term senior company executives as Dick Maurer, Bob Oppenlander, and even Hollis Harris.

Why was Beebe so certain after such a short period of time that Allen was the man he wanted or at least *thought* he wanted, to succeed him some day? It is my contention that, perhaps as much as anything else, Allen was a tool Beebe used to show his colleagues at Delta his utter contempt for them. Seniority, talent, experience, skill—in short, all rele-vant indices of management ability which might be used to develop Delta's future—fell before Beebe's championing of Allen. And nothing could have generated more ill will as universally as such capricious favoritism.

The Beebe-Dolson Clash

I remember one especially sharp stroke of the Beebe touch which occurred right at the very top. In typical patriarchal fashion, it is a hallowed tradition at Delta that the annual meeting of stockholders be held in Monroe, Louisiana, the fatherland where C.E. Woolman founded the company as a crop dusting outfit in 1928. But it is also characteristic of the way Delta manages its information flow and provides access to the decision-making process that these meetings are held in a relatively inaccessible place—like Monroe. The location was chosen to create a dampening effect for any corporate gadfly or dissident shareholder or unruly member of the Delta family who might wish to speak his or her piece.

Winging our way on a specially chartered DC-9 for the October, 1970 annual meeting, Beebe's first as chairman and chief executive officer, I remember standing in the aisle chatting with him about the parliamentary procedures for the meeting, when Beebe changed the subject and said with that ever-present crooked smile, "You'll never catch me around for as long as Dolson was around. When I hit 65 I'm gone. Men start losing it at 65, and you're not going to catch me around then. Dolson was losing it and had to be replaced."[1]

I may have been young, and I may have been naive, but this astonished me.

At a fateful January 1970 board meeting, Beebe had staged a coup which had dethroned Dolson as CEO and run roughshod over Richard Maurer, who up to that point had been considered a likely contender to succeed Dolson in due course.

Behind the scenes, Beebe had been lobbying hard and had persuaded the passive external board members—whose average age was over 70 and probably closer to 80—that Dolson had to go in order to preserve Delta's leadership position in the industry. Beebe capitalized on the lack of resolve of the external board members, and was unanimously elected president and chief executive officer. Dolson was relegated to the chairmanship of the board, with no day-to-day responsibilities.

Charlie Dolson was the kind of man who would come through the ranks and pick up for lunch anyone who cared to go down the street to Morrison's Cafeteria, on Virginia Avenue, near Delta's headquarters. Since I, among others, ate lunch with him at least two or three times a week, I noticed after the January board meeting that he became much more introspective and, in fact, made a point of not coming to the office every day. Dolson was a fine businessman who knew the airline industry intimately, and it was hard to see him laid so low by Beebe.

What was lost in that coup was not merely a leader but a style of leadership that was both humane and secure. In my opinion, when Dolson lost to Beebe, the company lost something vital that it has never recovered.

Unlike Beebe, Charlie Dolson was the kind of leader who gave Delta's managers and professionals as much opportunity for growth and experience as they could profit from.

One memorable example of Dolson's ability to encourage leadership across a broad range of his executive staff came several months after Rolls Royce Aero Engines Limited, the manufacturer of the RB-211 engines which were installed on the Lockheed L-1011 TriStars, went bankrupt. In January 1970, the Lockheed Corporation advised its L-1011 customers that it was in serious financial straits and the only way its commercial airplane venture could survive would be through some form of Congressional funding. Much debate raged over whether or not Congress should bail out a defense contractor which had attempted to re-enter the commercial aircraft market and fallen into serious difficulty. The L-1011 was the first and only commercial jet airliner Lockheed ever produced.

The debate raged in the Congress, and after several months, President Nixon instructed his Treasury Secretary, John Connally, to chair a meeting to be attended by the chairmen of the airlines who were L-1011 customers and who supported the concept of a Congressional bail out for Lockheed. It was, I remember, a few days before the meeting when Charlie Dolson came into my office and said, "Hell, Davis, you know more about this damn subject than I do. I want you to get your butt up to Washington and meet with Connally."

I still remember the exhilaration of that assignment from Dolson. Needless to say, it was quite an experience for a 34-year-old staff lawyer in a meeting filled with airline chairmen and their general counsels, to be seated right next to the Secretary of the Treasury.

Unlike Dolson, Beebe never seemed able to understand that responsible corporate leadership included the development of leadership potential in junior staff members. I suspect that Beebe was himself so insecure in his position that he could not bring himself to nurture those who might aspire to succeed him. In my view, Beebe's failing in this

regard contributed a mean spirit to Delta that at its base fed
upon that essential insecurity and weakness of character.

Politically, of course, Beebe made sure his position
was secure by focusing all his developmental energies on the
Allen fast track. In this way, he could depend on Allen's
absolute loyalty and support while, at the same time, undercut all other managers who might have had the talent and
the ambition to challenge him or his lineage for the leadership position. Delta has never overcome the weakness that
fact created in Beebe's peers or the lack of experience in
Allen's managerial talent.

Beebe on Discrimination

During the mid to late 1970s, the Labor Department, the
Justice Department and the Office of Federal Contracts Compliance Programs (OFCCO), were aggressively hunting
down large employers who had a profile of sexual, racial or
religious discrimination in their hiring and firing practices.
These companies were identified and put on what was
described as a "fast track" which gave them a high profile
with the Labor and Justice Departments and, if nothing else,
created job security for lawyers.

Delta was put on such a fast track, apparently due to
a pattern of class action lawsuits which had been filed in the
early 1970s by blacks and women, charging the company
with racial or sexual discrimination. Amazingly enough,
these suits generated very little publicity, which was a great
credit to Delta's ability to stroke the press. Failure to resolve
the fast track issues, on terms and conditions which the
company would have found to be extremely onerous, would
have inevitably resulted in a class action lawsuit by the
Justice Department.

It was during such a time, particularly at one point
when the relationship between Delta and the Office of
Federal Contracts Compliance Programs was becoming more
adversarial and less cooperative—carried to its fullest extent,
that would have meant referral to the Justice Department for
a pattern and practice lawsuit which would have consumed

millions of dollars of Delta's money—that Tom Beebe called one of the other lawyers and me into his office, apparently spontaneously. I was asked to join because I was responsible for supervising all of Delta's discrimination litigation from the law department side of the matter, and the other lawyer was a staff member working for me.

Unbelievably, Beebe started the meeting by telling us, notwithstanding the obvious trend and strong governmental pressure to the contrary, that the company would "... no longer hire any more male flight attendants, because they get restless, and restlessness creates unions. Besides," Beebe continued, "they are as gay as a three-dollar bill, and we don't need any fags in the Delta family."

Whether it was a draconian nature or profound, even abysmal ignorance of the real world that prompted such an unwarranted statement, I cannot say. I suspect the former, or, at best, that he might have developed permanent scar tissue from his earlier battles with the unions which did not permit him to think matters of this sort through rationally.

Beebe the Manager

During the last few years of his administration, Beebe pressed hard to put Allen in line to become Garrett's ultimate successor as chief executive officer. There was little doubt that Garrett would succeed Beebe, because he had a strong operations background. Moreover, because he was nearly ten years younger than Beebe, he was the right age. Allen, fresh out of Georgia Tech, was on a somewhat shakier ground because of his lack of experience.

Beebe closeted himself most of the time with Garrett, and later spent more and more time with both Garrett and Allen. He never took Oppenlander and Maurer, the other inside members of the board of directors, into his confidence: he preferred to consult them only on an as-needed basis. It was clear from Allen's ascension to the board and his expanded authority in the personnel and administration area that he was Beebe's heir apparent.

To his very great credit, Tom Beebe had a personal propaganda program that heavyweight Hollywood press

agents would have envied and admired, and which culmi-
nated in his selection in 1978 as the Gold Winner in the 1977
Chief Executive Officer of the Year competition sponsored
by *Financial World* Magazine. Beebe was described in the
attendant feature article as being "... at his desk before 7
o'clock most mornings."[2,3]

Like many other chief executives, Beebe projected the
kind of persona the company lavished its PR budget creating. So taken in were the editors at *Financial World* that
when they crowned Beebe with the Gold Award for Chief
Executive Officer of the Year, they wrote glowingly of his
management style as follows:

"Symbolically at least, the corporate style at Delta
seems to be set by the fact that it is one of the few major
corporations in America where the chairman's door is really
open to anyone who has a problem. 'My rug has to be
cleaned once a month,' Beebe chuckles. 'Mechanics, pilots,
flight attendants—they all come in to see me. If they really
want to tell us something, we'll give them the time. They
don't have to go through somebody. The chairman, the
president, the vice presidents—none of us has an administrative assistant to screen people out, an intermediary.
We're available.'"[4,5]

Throughout Beebe's tenure, and even today, the
notion of Delta being an open-door company is, on its face,
ludicrous. Once, under Woolman, when the company was
much smaller, there had been such a thing, but it was Beebe
himself who studiously deconstructed that policy as I have
described. That he should pretend that Delta was still that
little company where the CEO patriarch could permit any of
the nearly 50,000 employees to tell him about the problems
in the trenches underscores the strength of the Delta family
myth. Delta is as hierarchial and bound to its organizational
table as any other major company. Further, in discussions
about Beebe with employees at Delta, from senior executives
down to the managerial level, not one who served under
Tom Beebe remembers him as the patriarch that he would
have us believe he was.

I remember a story which appeared in the press about Beebe while he was chairman of the company and was flying somewhere or other, seated next to another executive of a large company. The executive later reported that "Beebe actually got tears in his eyes" as Beebe talked to him about "the Delta family."

Somehow I am reminded of Tammy Bakker.

Beebe in Retirement

The press release announcing Beebe's retirement in 1980, said that the chairman's office would be "... out of the hierarchy at Delta," but Beebe promised that he would be around for a long time, "... possibly as long as ten years. The company needs me as it is going through the deregulation phase." Beebe would be 75 years old in ten years. What was that about Charlie Dolson losing it at 65? Tom Beebe did retire, in January 1980, a few months before the *Financial World* article appeared, but stayed on as chairman of the board with an office at the company headquarters. Each retiring CEO of Delta since Dolson has been given an office on the premises to work out of post-retirement, which perpetuates the vestiges of a prior administration, for better or for worse. In Beebe's case, it was for the worst, for from that office Beebe continued in an ever-increasing tempo to criticize the senior management of the company, especially in 1982 when hard times and losses occurred.

"It never would have happened on my watch," Beebe would tell anyone he could corner. In my opinion, Beebe had no personal impact one way or the other on Delta's performance.

Finally, he went too far. For two years, he had vocalized the same subject, loudly, during board meetings so often that David Garrett grew tired of being increasingly second-guessed as chief executive officer of the company and forced a showdown with Beebe in front of the external board's directors. As a result, Beebe was given the option of retiring gracefully or being fired. Naturally, he chose the former and departed, in January 1982, unlamented.

Parting Shots

My own personal, parting experience with Beebe tells, I think, a compelling story about his character and about the myth of his leadership.

In August 1979 I accepted the position of general counsel of Springs Industries, Inc., and so wrote a joint memorandum announcing my resignation to David Garrett, Richard Maurer, who was then vice chairman of the board, and Tom Beebe.

It was a "done deal," as they say. As much as I dreaded the idea of giving up aviation, I had come to the conclusion that in my early 40s I was at a relative dead end at Delta. I had also begun to feel increasingly uneasy in the presence of Messrs. Beebe and Allen, with their unyielding way of second-guessing decisions made by staff professionals as well as by operations people. Then, too, I viewed them both as intellectually dishonest men, fickle in their judgments and capricious in their decisions, particularly as they affected the career paths of the more visible Delta managers.

Garrett had done his share in convincing me, too. When I was elected to the board of directors of the prestigious Metropolitan Atlanta Area Crime Commission, founded by former Attorney General Griffin Bell, it came back to me directly that Garrett was very upset that the matter had not been cleared through him personally. This was typically of Delta's unwillingness, at least at that time, to support and encourage participation by Delta officers in worthwhile local affairs.

Both Garrett and Maurer invited me to their offices, and each was gracious in wishing me well. I was particularly pleased that Garrett paid me the ultimate compliment of being a "damned fine lawyer." I was more touched by Dick Maurer, though, when he said that he was losing a personal friend in the work place.

I waited uneasily, for two hours, in fact, for the call from Beebe. I was the first vice president who had voluntarily resigned from Delta in the history of the company and wasn't sure what kind of reception I would get from Beebe. The matter was soon resolved.

"You god damn bastard!" said Beebe, smiling that nonstop smile and waving his copy of my resignation memorandum. "You god damn bastard," he repeated.

Suddenly, I was overwhelmed with relief at what I had just done. I said, "Thank you, Tom, my mother particularly thanks you, but you are so good about all this bullshit you throw around about the Delta family, I thought you might be a little more cordial and perhaps even understanding."

Ignoring my observation (and my mother's thanks), Beebe continued, smiling, "You *will* at least have to stay until after the annual meeting.

I wasn't sure what he was driving at, but I had planned to be aboard my new company on October 15, which was about ten days before Delta's annual meeting date. "How so?" I asked.

"Your name is in the proxy statement, and we can't be changing it at the Securities and Exchange Commission and mailing it again to all our stockholders because it's too damned expensive," he said.

I was really curious now. Delta always prepared and printed its proxy statement in-house, and if modifying that was a problem, I didn't see it.

"I'm not sure I understand, Tom," I responded.

Obviously impatient with my ignorance, Beebe went on to say, "Well, your god damned name is in the proxy statement because you are on the proxy committee and I don't think it is fair of you to leave early so that the company has to go to all that expense in changing it."

The light went on: Beebe, for seven years chairman of the board, still didn't understand the procedures for chairing an annual meeting. Maurer had to spoon-feed him every year. It was pathetic.

"Wait a minute, Tom," I said. "I think you are a little confused. *You* are on the proxy committee, but *I'm not*. I'm one of the inspectors of election, but my name doesn't appear in the proxy statement.

Looking visibly relieved, Beebe told me to "Get the hell out of here, then." Beebe never spoke to me again, although we had several encounters both before and after my departure from Delta.

Chapter Nine

The Wrong Stuff

It is an immutable law in business
that words are words, explanations
are explanations, promises are
promises—but only performance is
reality.
—Harold S. Geneen

Send in the Clones

When I think about the way in which Beebe nurtured
Ronald W. Allen's career and set him on the managerial
stage at Delta, it occurs to me that Delta has been ill-served
by such patronage. Allen is a complete anomaly as an airline
executive. His only experience is derived from Delta—he is
the pure son of an impure corporate father; one of those
men of the new age, fashioned from malleable clay, trained,
groomed and nurtured to be scion of Delta. Yet for Delta, I
suspect, Ron Allen is the wrong man at the wrong time.
Unless he has enormous undetected powers of growth, the
wisdom to admit his mistakes and seek advice from beyond
Delta, then I suspect he will, like Beebe, maintain the status
quo of management in a self-styled vacuum. Since he will
probably be chairman of the board and chief executive
officer of the company until the year 2008, we should take
the measure of the man, if we are to assess Delta's chances
for the future.

As we have seen in the previous chapter, the careers
of Tom Beebe and Ron Allen are inextricably bound together.
In a way, it is unfortunate to rise through the management
ranks as a result of patronage, because patronage not only
denies an individual's right to rise on this own merits but
also denies him the right to fail. In the end, patronage will

often produce managers who cannot be forceful without being vindictive and who cannot be decisive without being rigid. When the patron is also the mentor, the growth so nurtured is often characterized by imitation rather than by maturation. When the patron/mentor was Tom Beebe, well ... the results are not likely to be those one would admire.

Mirror, Mirror ...

In Ronald Allen's case, it is interesting to see how much like the corporate father this son has become. Like Beebe, Allen is not much liked by the rank and file at Delta. In fact, Allen is intensely disliked by the large majority of the pilot group. Although Allen himself would surely tell you that Frank Rox is to blame, Allen is widely regarded as the culprit who caused so much bitterness in recent negotiations with pilots. Management's intractability actually forced these negotiations into mediation and backed the pilots into such a predicament that they refused to fly overtime. It was the first time in the history of Delta that such acrimony has existed between Delta management and its pilot group.

From another point of view, however, the mere fact that the pilot group doesn't like Allen may actually mean that he is doing his job well. Surely, any airline's CEO would want to protect his company against further erosion of costs by refusing to increase the wages of the highest-paid pilot group in the United States.

The Paradigm Case

At the time Allen took over the reins, a number of people within the company felt that he was not tested in the marketplace. Indeed, in telling me of their concerns at that time, they observed how odd it was that Allen had not yet made a major decision which could have a material impact, either favorably or unfavorably, on the company. The board of directors apparently were aware of this unknown quality in Allen's potential leadership and so to fend off the possibility of any misstep, they elected Dave Garrett to become chairman of the executive committee—with the strong admonition that he continue to stay active. They were especially insistent that Garrett remain involved in the management of the operational end of the business in general and, more specifically, in the oversight of aircraft fleet selection.

Garrett's presence and availability may together comprise a vital crutch for Allen, but the combination suggests that the guard has not really changed at Delta. The company is in for more of the same: in tandem, Garrett and Allen share the same old paradigm of the same old guard and will not risk innovation merely for the sake of innovation.

A Clean Slate

On the other hand, the middle managers at Delta, one or two rungs down from Allen, genuinely seem to like him and think that he will do good things for Delta, given time and the opportunity. There is a unanimous feeling among these same managers that Garrett quite literally smothered the company during his tenure. Nowhere is this more true, they believe, than in the marketing arena. Allen, they contend, should not share the blame for Garrett's past mistakes, at least for the time being.

On the Fast Track

Allen's rise at Delta should stand as the epitome of the fast track. There has never been such speedy ascension in the senior management ranks at Delta.

- In 1963, Allen was hired as a staff analyst in the methods and training section of the personnel department;
- From 1966-1967 he served as director of methods and training;
- For two years, 1967-1968, he served as assistant vice president of administration;
- In 1969, Allen was named vice president, an event unprecedented event in Delta's history;
- One year later, in 1970, Allen was named senior vice president of personnel to succeed Beebe when Beebe became chairman of the board. An even more startling promotion.

• Then, in 1983 Allen was named president and chief operating officer of Delta, the apparent if not obvious heir to Dave Garrett.

For some reason, I keep wanting to ask, as they often do in the comic books, "What's wrong with this picture?" Two things are wrong. First, in a complete perversion of the promotion-from-within policy, Beebe elevated an untried and untested member of his own personnel department over wiser, better trained, more experienced and more capable individuals. In the process, he permitted the complete demoralization of an entire generation of managers who had led the company to its success. Second, like Beebe, Allen had gained most of his experience in the personnel department, a department grounded in the disciplines of psychology and statistics, not in finance or marketing or any of the other traditional disciplines which form the basis of the airline industry. Historically, personnel departments have always been ancillary units—service units which facilitate the work of the operations managers but which, in themselves, are not profit centers and as such are generally unequipped with the expertise which drives the business or industry. In my opinion, the elevation of a personnel specialist to chief executive officer status is questionable in the extreme and dangerous to the health of any industrial or manufacturing enterprise.

More to the point, in Delta's case, is that in the deregulated environment, marketing skills have begun to be the dominant expertise required of executive officers. Delta will probably live or die by Ron Allen's marketing prowess. The problem is, however, he has no marketing background. His entire experience has been at Delta and, as a consequence, he has no marketing tradition to draw upon. Worse yet, he seems reluctant to swim against the strong anti-marketing bias that has historically characterized the Delta mind set. I wonder, in fact, if Allen would even recognize a state-of-the-art marketing program if he saw it.

Playing Hardball

During the period I worked at Delta, Allen and I had a very cordial working relationship, though I confess he always seemed somewhat naive about what I am pleased to call "the real world," that is to say, the world outside Delta. For example, over the course of longstanding discussions with the OFCCP about Delta's alleged discriminatory attitude regarding women and minorities, Allen always instructed the lawyers to "play hard ball," without any flexibility at all, to negotiate a reasonable middle-of-the-road settlement posture. I always felt that this attitude unnecessarily exacerbated the relationship between the OFCCP and Delta. It is not surprising, to me, that as a direct result of his attitude, the investigation, which started ten years ago, has only closed its books this past year.

Let's Do Lunch

It was always my impression that the senior officers, particularly Bob Oppenlander and Dick Maurer, only politely tolerated Allen as a peer when he became senior vice president. I would have had to be very insensitive not to notice that they both seemed to think it was ludicrous when he was elected to the board of directors, 11 years out of college.

Hold My Calls, Please

In 1976, Margaret Ann Thornberry, an agent in the reservations office of Delta Air Lines in San Francisco, filed a lawsuit under Title VII of the Civil Rights Act of 1964, alleging that she had been denied promotion by the company on a basis which discriminated against her on account of her sex. The case was assigned to the Honorable Robert Peckham, a federal district judge in San Francisco. Peckham had the reputation of being a fair but extremely liberal judge when it came to employees or former employees doing battle against employers or, for that matter, to any concern proscribed by the Civil Rights Act.

I was the lead in the Delta strategy for defending the case and Hunter Hughes, senior attorney, was assigned to it from the Delta staff as well. Hunter, who later left Delta for private practice, is a tenacious lawyer with few peers in his field, but at that time he was a young and a relatively inexperienced civil rights defense lawyer. We hired a very fine law firm in San Francisco and began defending the case. After a series of hearings and oral arguments, Judge Peckham certified the case as a class action, which meant that every former employee, employee applicant, or current employee of Delta who felt that [he or] she had been discriminated against on the basis of sex was free to enter the case as a plaintiff along with Ms. Thornberry. The claim for damages was in the millions, and I remember very well that the lead counsel for Ms. Thornberry bought a Mercedes during the course of the litigation; she obviously thought she knew something we didn't.

The case drew itself out over a couple of years, and so, in the normal routine of such litigation, I had to make numerous trips to San Francisco. Normally, we traveled on the weekends, and as anyone with a young family can testify, this kind of schedule was no fun. Frankly, San Francisco is great for a long weekend, but when you have been there as long as we were, it turns to concrete and water pretty quickly.

After plodding along for almost two years, the Thornberry case was approaching the time for trial setting. About this time, Ms. Thornberry's lawyers suggested to the judge that perhaps they might be interested in some type of out-of-court settlement. We replied, cautiously, that we would be willing to enter into such discussions, but we needed time to check with management regarding acceptable terms of settlement.

Consequently, we returned to Atlanta and discussed the matter with Ron Allen, who was then the senior vice president of personnel. It was decided that Hughes and I would return to California and try to work out a satisfactory settlement, one which would allow Delta to maintain a low profile, and we were urged to try to keep the settlement as economical as possible. Into this narrative I should enter the fact that the plaintiffs had been able to produce evidence during pretrial concerning the treatment of Ms. Thornberry which was fairly negative for Delta, although the company also had some strong defenses about its reasons for her denial of promotion.

Nevertheless, on the day before Hunter and I were to return to San Francisco, I was called into Ron Allen's office. After we reviewed some general issues of the Thornberry case, Ron surprised me by saying, "Sid, it's time you started acting like a vice president."

I am sure the silence wasn't as long as it seemed at the time, but during that silence, I was trying to figure out just exactly what Ron had in mind.

Half-kiddingly, I replied, "Well, Ron, perhaps you can tell me what a vice president should be acting like."

It then became obvious that he was very serious, as he began to criticize my frequent trips to the West coast to participate in the Thornberry case. After assuring him that I did not enjoy traveling half the weekend, my daughters were young, and that San Francisco had lost its charm for me, I then asked him what he thought I was doing that was wrong.

Without responding directly, he said, "Well, vice presidents in this company are supposed to sit in their office, wait for telephone calls from their subordinates and then make decisions which the subordinates carry out."

I think I would have been laughing if the matter was not such an economically sensitive one for Delta at the time.

"Well," I tried to explain, "we are, as you know, at a very sensitive point in negotiations in the Thornberry case, and I really feel like we need a decision-maker on the scene, at least a person one tier removed from the final decision, to reason out whether or not any settlement offer is worth passing on to management. For that reason alone, I think it is worth a trip to the West Coast."

"But you have Hunter Hughes out there to make those recommendations to you," Allen replied.

Now it must be said that I had negotiated a lot of contracts, a lot of deals and had, in fact, settled more than a few cases. It was my considered opinion then, as it is today, that there is nothing like a face-to-face encounter with the enemy, particularly when you are entering into settlement negotiations. After explaining this belief to Ron, I was nevertheless advised to terminate my plans to go to San Francisco and ordered to work with Hunter "... on the telephone."

Somewhere in the personnel office I am sure there must have been a job description called "vice president" which described a quasi-electronic potentate who made Solomon-like decisions via telephone. The words, "act like a vice president," rang in my ears as I went out of Allen's office to telephone my duly considered acceptance to the chairman of Springs Industries who had offered me the position of general counsel.

It wouldn't surprise me to learn that Ron Allen still dispenses this infantile advice at Delta today, because nothing that he has experienced or been exposed to during the several years since that conversation has likely had any impact on his perspective of the way a vice president should act or, for that matter, how any other member of the management team should act. His one-dimensional understanding of the responsibility of key players is at once astonishing and alarming.

Status Quo Vadis

When Delta first looked at Western in August 1984, Western had a market value of approximately $65 million. Bill Farrell, a vice president at Kidder, Peabody & Co., Inc. in New York and formerly vice president corporate planning and finance at Western, was surprised at how cautious Delta's approach to acquiring Western was. "During the course of the negotiations," says Farrell, "Oppenlander repeatedly referred to the fact that Delta had been able to acquire Northeast at half the asking price, expecting us to fall on bended knee, I think—which was a joke. We weren't dummies, and knew that Northeast was only six weeks away from bankruptcy when Delta acquired it in 1972 and that we were a player for keeps by the time the negotiations with Delta really got serious.

"In a word, I don't think we really needed Delta. Lloyd Jones [Western's COO at the time] was busy lining up interline agreements with other carriers. We were ready to move ahead," Farrell said.

Finally, when Delta asked for "a second look," Western officials made it clear that no external circumstances such as fuel price changes which might affect earnings, could affect the valuation of Western and that the only change could be occasioned by some management transaction which was inept and might materially affect the price of the company.

Delta bought off on Western's demands, and the rest is history: Delta paid approximately $900 million two years after it began looking at Western. This was well over ten times the price that it could have been bought for when Delta began looking. According to Delta's *1987 Annual Report to Stockholders*, the total cost of the Western acquisition exceeded the preliminary valuation of the underlying net assets of Western by $413 million![1] If ever there were cause for amazement, it is that little-known fact.

Farrell turned down an offer to become an officer of Delta, "Because," he says, "my sense of it was that the company was so parochial that I would never get anywhere, since I was not incubated in the Delta mode from day one of my career."

Delta's decision to buy Western Air Lines was, according to close observers, a totally reactionary undertaking and by no means any indication of a new or bold management style. When Delta started looking at Western, as early as early 1985, the per-share price of Western stock was at the $6 level.

Ron Allen led the battle against the acquisition of Western and was supported by Olin Galloway in this opposition. Both Allen and Galloway felt that as Western was then emerging from some rather severe financial difficulties, its acquisition would be too expensive. After almost a year of tortuous deliberation, pro-Western forces at Delta prevailed, and the board agreed to purchase Western for a price which was over ten times the market price of Western when Delta had begun its early "sniff tests." In fact, just before the merger plans were announced, many observers in the financial community speculated that because the price of Western had doubled, not only was it well over-valued, mostly due to the merger rumors, but also that it would be a serious mistake for Delta to buy it at such an inflated price.

Ron Allen led the conservative element within the company, arguing for the status quo. In this case, Allen was probably right for the wrong reasons: Western has not yet produced positive economic benefits for Delta, although it has enabled the company to expand its Western horizons within the United States. The notion that Ron Allen was sophisticated enough to see that Western might not produce positive benefits early on is suspect; it seems much more likely to me that he opted for the status quo.

Media Blitzed

In recent years, there have been a number of commentaries on Delta's management, particularly as the transition from Garrett to Allen took place. Some of the observers of the transition were neutral, but the majority of them suggested that Delta might not be up to the challenge ahead. One analyst remarked, for example, that "... in tapping Mr. Allen, [as chairman and chief executive officer] Delta continues its long tradition of promoting only from within its own ranks of mostly Southern-bred managers. Like Mr. Garrett, he took a degree from Georgia Institute of Technology. The Atlanta-born Mr. Allen started working part-time for Delta twenty-four years ago as an under-graduate. Mr. Harris [the new president and chief operating officer] fits the mold as well, as a native of Carrollton, Ga., who also graduated from Georgia Tech."[2]

Edward Starkman, an airline analyst with Paine Webber, called Allen "a typical Delta manager: mild mannered, knows his business and is a Southern Delta gentleman."[3] An *Atlanta Journal* business writer had this to say about the pending retirement of David Garrett as chairman and chief executive officer: "Dramatic change is not something that analysts have come to fear from Delta's management. Quite the contrary, one of the few criticisms analysts have levied against the airline's leadership in recent years is that it has been so deeply entrenched that it has become stodgy."

"There has been some concern that they [Delta] haven't been aggressive enough in keeping up with changes in the industry," one airline analyst said, citing Delta's historical reluctance to respond to fare-based competition, for example. "There is some feeling that they [Delta's top management] may still be an old gentlemen's club."[4]

Indeed, Allen does preside over an elite club of nine top corporate officers who run Delta on a day-to-day basis. On average, each has spent 32.6 years with the company; Russell H. Heil, senior vice president of personnel, is the neophyte of the group with 21 years at Delta. The "grand-daddy" is senior vice president—finance and administration M.O. Galloway, who joined Delta in 1945 as a timekeeper. Contrary to what one might expect for a group who have given their adult lives to Delta, Allen's private club is not very peaceful. The senior member of the club, Galloway, believing himself to be less well compensated than he deserved, recently stomped out of the corporate offices.

Although Ron Allen is only the fifth chief executive officer in Delta's 60-year history, the average tenure is not as long as that might suggest, because Woolman ran the company for the first 38 years.

On the Short Track

During his stint as Delta's chief operating officer, Allen was largely overshadowed by Dave Garrett, so it is difficult to critically assess what kind of company Allen might leave behind—assuming he retires at normal retirement date in the year 2008 and that there is a company left to assess—except to extrapolate on his experience in rising through the ranks of the company. His is not a particularly reassuring record.

Just days before he became chief executive officer in August 1987, Allen sent an internal memo to "all members of the Delta family" admitting the operational mishaps that had occurred over the previous month. In that memo, subsequently circulated by Whit Hawkins, the senior vice president—marketing, to Delta Frequent Flyer program participants, Allen wrote, "How do we as individual members of the Delta family respond to this negative reflection on our company? How do we answer questions from the customers whom we are privileged to serve? How do we react to the media, our neighbors, our friends, etc., who wonder if something has changed at Delta? There is only one way we can respond—to be clear that Delta has not changed...."

Allen's very cautious, sometimes negative attitude about the Western merger and the time that it took to consummate that transaction, at tenfold increased cost to Delta, seem to confirm Allen's penchant for maintaining the status quo.

Lip Service

In addition to receiving high marks for his marketing skills from the press, Allen is also being touted as the first Delta executive to become active in civic affairs in the Atlanta community since he now occupies the position of chairman-elect of the Atlanta Chamber of Commerce. What has *not* been heralded in Atlanta is his departure from the very effective and important downtown Rotary Club. As soon as he became chief executive officer at Delta, Allen resigned from the Rotary Club and several important role playing committees, although he did retain the rather ceremonial title of chairman-elect of the chamber.

"I was very disappointed in him," says retired Lieutenant General Collier Ross, former Commanding General of the U.S. Third Army, who had been looking forward to drawing on Allen's back-ground in the personnel area to move one of his committees in the Rotary along.

There has been a dearth of active participation by Delta officials in civic affairs around Atlanta. Some observers offered an apology for Garrett on the basis that Delta is now a worldwide company with worldwide operations and stockholders dispersed everywhere so Garrett is too busy to play in the local community. That, to me, is a complete whitewash. No company is more international and more involved at every employee level in civic affairs than the Coca-Cola Company, headquartered in Atlanta. Similarly, Georgia Pacific, which moved to Atlanta about ten years ago and has worldwide operations, is actively visible in the community. The way I see it, employees of Delta, from top management down through the lowest ranks, don't like to mingle outside the company.

The Bunker Mentality

In the fall of 1987 in the midst of all the bad press regarding airline flight delays, *The Atlanta Journal and Constitution* ran a small piece on the fact that "Delta's record for late flights was among [the] worst in September."[5] Shortly thereafter, a letter appeared in the letters to the editor of *The Atlanta Journal* on November 19, 1987, under the headline, in boldface type, "Why Denigrate Delta?" The letter said, "I ask you simply why you have taken yet another opportunity [others were not described] to attempt to denigrate the record of a Company which contributes as much to the City of Atlanta as Delta does?"[6]

The letter was signed by T. Hunter Ewing of Atlanta. Mr. Ewing is the son of the former director of public relations for Delta. To say that he, understandably, is a Delta loyalist is to miss the obvious: More likely, young Mr. Ewing's letter expresses an attitude drawn directly from the corporate environment Mr. Allen both nurtures and is sustained by.

It is worth examining the points of the letter as it indicates how emotional the reaction to what is perceived as bad press is—and how unrelated to reality. For example, it is hard to see how the article denigrated Delta by simply pointing out, from information filed by Delta itself, that the company had indeed, as it consistently does, "...one of the worst on time records...." in the airline industry in the United States.[7]

In regard to the other issue Mr. Ewing decries, the contribution that Delta makes to Atlanta, his complaint is not specific. Does he mean payroll? Of course, Delta's payroll makes a meaningful economic contribution to the Atlanta metropolitan area, but there is more to a big company than payroll. There is time. Executives who contribute their time and their expertise to community affairs are a large component of what a company contributes to the city where it is headquartered. Delta makes few such contributions; perhaps its relatively remote location makes it difficult. Delta's corporate headquarters are located south of Atlanta, and its fortress-like office complex is near the airport but isolated from everything and everyone else.

One afternoon, during a discussion with a partner in one of Atlanta's most prominent law firms, the issue of community service surfaced, prompting him to remark, "I sense in Delta sort of a 'siege mentality.' I used to see some of the lawyers like yourself, Sid, at the Atlanta Bar meetings, but beyond that, Delta has a zero profile in the city. Like I said, maybe it is a siege mentality."

For years, Delta enjoyed the benefit of the doubt from the media. It was often said, at least in Atlanta, that in terms of the press, Delta brought out the worst in Eastern—and Eastern brought out the best in Delta. But two factors have developed in this decade which have made the going in this regard a little more difficult for Delta.

The first is the surprise that Delta has given Wall Street in its operating earnings over a period of several years. Nevertheless, this has not discouraged the investment community from the kind of hyperbole which describes Ron Allen as a "marketing wizard" and the like.

What has really changed the relationship with the press is the way Delta has handled certain operational matters and the lack of response by its senior management to the issues raised by these matters.

Take, for example, the matter of Delta's Flight 191: In September 1985, Flight 191, on an approach to Dallas-Ft. Worth Airport, encountered a wind shear turbulence which resulted in the crash of an L-1011 in which 137 people perished.

Immediately after the crash, Delta received the expected kid-glove treatment from the media for the way it handled notification of next of kin and the supporting efforts that were made by Delta employees on the scene to allow the devastated mourners the privacy to grieve. Later, however, as the inevitable litigation was initiated by survivors claiming wrongful death actions against Delta, Lockheed and the Federal government, some nasty little surprises came to light. During the resulting furor, Delta completely fumbled the media ball.

The first was a series of articles in national newspapers, charging that Delta's lawyers and its aviation insurance underwriting firm had engaged in scandalous conduct in attempts to reduce—or in fact eliminate—settlement claims by some of the survivors. For example, it was suggested that the insurance company reached the outrageous conclusions that because a young man who died on the flight was a bachelor in his late 30s, he was undoubtedly an AIDS victim. Other less scandalous allegations were made, but they still received national attention. And Delta did nothing!

Moreover, when the company was castigated for thirty minutes on CBS's *60 Minutes*, Delta eschewed its right to respond. As the saying goes, if it looks like the siege mentality, sounds like the siege mentality, and feels like the siege mentality, then it probably *is* the siege mentality.

As a former lawyer on Delta's staff, I believe it is entirely possible that the company probably had no idea what its insurance company was doing until the facts were made public. Although I must say that while I have personally received the instructions to play hardball from Allen, I would not like to think that this represents a new level of the kind of hardball Delta has chosen to play. If Delta did not know what the insurance company was doing, then we must ask why Delta did not totally disavow the outrageous conduct of its insurance company and its lawyers promptly and vociferously.

Nearly three years after the crash and after a number of claims were settled, Delta filed a lawsuit against the U.S.

Government and its Federal Aviation Administration. The lawsuit charged that the government was totally culpable for the crash of Flight 191 for two reasons: First, for its agents' careless conduct in failing to report the volatile storm conditions around the Dallas-Ft. Worth Airport to the airliner and, second, the control tower's failure to advise the crew of Flight 191 that there was actually a wind shear over the approach runway it intended to use. The government has alleged that the cause of the accident was the negligence of Delta's pilots in failing to perform a proper approach as they entered the turbulence, several moments before the actual wind shear was encountered.

Still ongoing at the time of this writing, the trial has been an almost daily media event. Although the judge has not yet ruled on the liability issues, it is my observation that this is a no-win situation for Delta. Why, then, I wonder, did Delta not join the Government on a cost-sharing basis to settle all of the remaining claims? To do so would have been a one-time event which, I believe, would have generated considerable good will among those who follow the case. Delta could have put an end to the deliberations, allowed the families of the deceased to get on with their lives and Delta to get on with business—all of which would have been proclaimed by the media as Delta's having done the right thing.

But what did Delta do? Played hardball, so that Atlanta and the nation were subjected to an almost daily melodrama in which the survivors and the witnesses needlessly had to endure a grim reenactment of the occasion which caused such profound grief. If negative media time were dollars, Delta is deeply in the red. I must say that whoever is coaching this game of legal hardball is giving Delta extremely poor counsel.

Seldom a company to be very consistent in any issue, Delta has recently confused all observers in this case. In a Massachusetts court, Delta paid the largest judgment ever awarded to a single individual in an airline crash case by compensating the family of an IBM executive who was killed in the Dallas crash.

Playing Dodge Ball

When he became chairman of the board in early August 1987, Ron Allen declined interviews with all newswire reporting services and the local newspapers. To do so was certainly his privilege, and if that reflects on a quiet, modest management style, then that, too, is fine. In this case, however, there were some other circumstances which suggest to me that Allen made a monumental error in refusing to be interviewed by the press and, indeed, in making press releases on his own.

Shortly before he became chairman, there were five operational incidents involving Delta air crews beginning with the captain of a Boeing B-767 cutting off both the aircraft engines on departure from Los Angeles to Cincinnati while climbing over the Pacific Ocean. Other incidents included two occasions of landing at the wrong airport or using the wrong runway at the right airport. Most telling, however, was the incident involving Delta Flight 37 en route from London to Cincinnati, an L-1011 TriStar, which nearly collided with a Continental B-747 while both aircraft were over the Atlantic.

In each of the incidents, the lives of everyone on each of the aircraft, passengers and air crew alike, were threatened and at stake. After the investigation of the several incidents, the Federal Aviation Administration issued a report severely criticizing Delta as being the recipient of "... one of the harshest F.A.A. criticisms of a major airline's flight operations" and charged that "Delta lacked clear management policies on crew training and coordination."[8]

On September 18, 1987, the Federal Aviation Administration issued a 35-page report, rife with descriptions of inadequacies in Delta training and operations. However, Delta had earlier issued its own news release about the inspection, titled, "Delta Procedures Meet and Exceed FAA Requirements."[9] The FAA had planned to release its report the following week, but, caught off guard, hurriedly distributed its own document. Not the least of the FAA's reasons for the early release of its report was to demonstrate the general misrepresentation inherent in Delta's news release which alleged that the first sentence of the FAA report indicated that the agency had found Delta to be in "general compliance with federal air regulations."[10]

Delta's press release never made reference to the report's second sentence, which said, "However, the team observed instances of a breakdown of communications, a lack of crew coordination and lapses of discipline in Delta's cockpits."[11]

Delta's self-serving article went on to quote chairman Allen as saying, "We welcomed the F.A.A. team's visit, and consider their report to be a conscientious and professional effort, and will use this resource to fine-tune and further strengthen our operation."[12]

The words "fine tune," "conscientious" and "professional" are merely buzz words at Delta, and this outrageous statement by Allen reflects a shallow and irresponsible response to a series of life-threatening events—each clearly caused by pilot error. If a procedure for shutting down engines over the Pacific Ocean with a load of passengers needs "fine tuning," please deliver the rest of us from whatever a "rough tuning" might be. "Fine tuning," indeed!

Such is the nature of the siege, or bunker, mentality which Allen and company have put to work at Delta. The passengers on those flights and shareholders of Delta should be outraged that this is the only comment which the company has ever formally issued through its chairman about those incidents.

All other comments issued by Delta on this issue were made at a lower, non-officer level. All such reports made it clear that the operational incidents were "internal matters" which would be dealt with through normal Delta procedures.

"We're a straight-arrow operation," said Delta spokesman Jim Ewing. "It's like the Boy Scouts getting in trouble, and we are working hard to get to the bottom of it...What's so frustrating is we can't tell you what we've found wrong other than human error."[13]

Frustrating? Is it possible that the reasons for these incidents could be anything other than human error? Does *human* error connote something less damnable than *pilot* error? Ewing's analogy to the Boy Scouts, although unintentional, not only indicates the attitude at Delta that they somehow fly with the angels but also makes one question whether Delta is aware of that familiar motto, "Be Prepared."

On Biting the Bullet

Coincidentally, in the summer of 1987, when Delta's problems were coming to a head, the Chrysler Corporation had its own problems. The Justice Department initiated criminal proceedings against Chrysler, alleging that Chrysler had regularly turned back the odometers on some of company's executive cars which were then sold as new cars. That was certainly a cheap and deceitful thing to do, albeit obviously not life-threatening. Lee Iacocca, chairman of Chrysler, reacted swiftly and decisively, saying: "We made mistakes that we will never make again. Period."

By owning up to a serious problem and publicly making amends, Iacocca turned a potential corporate disaster into a veritable public relations triumph. He simply did not hedge.

To be sure, the difference between Delta's handling of grave, life-threatening matters and Chrysler's handling of its own problems is vast, both in subjective nature and in demonstrated styles of leadership. Still, the question is raised: which reeks of integrity and which one does not?

A Blue Yonder

As I see it, projecting Ronald Allen's leadership of Delta into the next century is problematic, to say the least. There is little evidence that he is the manager who can lead Delta through the fiscal mine field it is surely approaching. His mastery of the media, like his mastery of the negotiation process, is nearly nil. His ability to handle crisis is demonstrably weak, and his support from his peers will steadily erode as long as he is unable to deal with the increasing structural weakness of his enterprise.

It seems to me that the hallmark of Allen's contribution to Delta, to date, is its utter lack of distinction. His stewardship is merely the logical end result of attempting to groom a man for management requiring very real superlatives by artificial processes. In Allen's case, the hothouse environment in which Beebe nurtured his career shielded him from the kinds of experience which create either superior strengths or wisdom. After Beebe's departure from the scene, Allen had acquired such momentum that none could challenge his ascension to Delta's corporate throne.

The jury is still out.

Chapter Ten

R$_x$ Delta

A miss? Or do my arrows hit the mark?
Or am I a quack prophet who knocks at doors, a babbler?
Give me your oath, confess I have the facts,
The ancient history of this house's crimes.
—Cassandra, in
The Agamemnon of Aeschylus

The Cassandra Complex

One of Homer's most memorable creations in *The Iliad*, one
which is retold by Aeschylus in his tragedy, *Agamemnon*, is
the tragic figure of Cassandra, the daughter of fabled Troy's
King Priam. A priestess of Apollo, Cassandra once fell
asleep in the temple and was awakened by Apollo, who
offered her the gift of prophecy if she would sleep with him.
She accepted his gift but spurned his bed. Apollo could not
take back his gift, but he could render it worthless. Consequently, whenever Cassandra correctly foretold the future no
one would believe it. As I write this book, the one thing that
gives me greatest pause is that, like Cassandra, I may be
able to give the problem Delta faces form and substance, but
because it is I who has done so, that naming will be
disregarded. Worse yet, the very problems I name and the
solutions I pose will by my naming and proposing be
immediately ruled out of any serious consideration of how
to resolve Delta's predicament.

Nevertheless, as I have named the problems Delta
faces in this book I must also name potential ways Delta
could resolve them, for my real intent in writing is saluta-
tory, and hence I must propose a cure for the illness I sense
behind these symptoms.

165

Get Outside Help

A few years ago, American Airlines hired a major U.S. consulting firm to do an analysis of its organizational charts and make recommendations on how to trim excess staff in the airline and posture the company for, using president and chief executive officer Bob Crandall's own description, the continuation of "legalized warfare in the industry."

The consulting firm made several recommendations regarding staffing. For example, it recommended that the current CFO at that time should take over the function of treasurer of the company, pointing out that substantial savings could be realized by folding what was then a bifurcated job into one position. Similarly Delta has an individual who has the position of vice president and treasurer and another who serves as vice president and chief financial officer. While there is no suggestion that the job of treasurer is a redundant one, there is a suspicion there. The consulting firm also helped American fashion a strategy for implementing an early retirement program for redundant executives by making some fairly irresistible one-time cash offers which did not count towards final average earnings for calculation of retirement income.

The consulting firm also evaluated American's business strategy in light of diversifying from airline and computerized reservations systems endeavors into other, perhaps travel-related, endeavors such as United had once done. The consulting firm told American to "stick to its knitting" and do what it knows how to do best: move passengers and freight by airplanes.

There is no stigma attached to hiring an expert consulting firm and listening carefully to its advice, although such advice may in some cases be strong medicine and even repugnant to, say, those who cling to established paternalistic policies, as is the case at Delta. Nevertheless, that Delta's chairman of the board has privately admitted to at least one former Western official that it is "overstaffed" can be interpreted as a desperate plea, however oblique, for help and direction in fashioning a remedy for the over-staffed malaise. If a substantial reduction in personnel at Delta will help them spread the margins between operating income and operating expenses, then—regardless of how unpalatable it may be at first glance—the medicine should be digested and Delta should get about the business of becoming a leaner airline.

As I have already mentioned, a number of young, mid-level professionals on the various staffs at Delta are seeking opportunities elsewhere. There is no better way to curb that loss of talent and the expenses associated with training it than by turning the professional jobs into self-starting ones which clearly define career paths for each advancement in grade. A bureaucratic culture simply has no place in the free-for-all called deregulation.

Control the Controllables

Delta has to do more than wallpaper its controllable expenses with accounting changes. There is only one way to improve the margins between operating income and operating expenses, and that is to cut real dollars out of the expense side of the ledger. One obvious way to do that is to address the issue of salaries and staffing head on.

Delta brags incessantly about its lack of labor unions, but even now there are rumblings of employee dissatisfaction, particularly among those older employees who have received what they view to be less than satisfactory wage increases over the past several years. This is a tough business in a tough industry, even in good times, so perhaps Delta should seize the one big advantage that a non-unionized work force has: fire the dissidents. Without an inspired maneuver which diffuses its rigid no-layoff or reduced-wage policy, this explosive segment of the overhead continues to imply impending disaster.

Apparently, there has been no challenge to the no-layoff policy from any intellectual perspective at any level within the company at any time. It is astonishing, to me, that even Bob Oppenlander, chief financial officer of the company for nearly 30 years, publicly repeated his dedication to not only upholding the no-layoff policy but also to paying the highest wages possible to secure the best people possible, regardless of what rate of return such an investment might generate for the welfare of Delta's stockholders.

Demonstrate Financial Stewardship

For many years, Oppenlander was viewed in the industry as the prototype investment banker turned airline CFO. I saw quite a different picture.

Mention has already been made of the vicarious way the decision was reached to agree upon a 6.5 percent fixed-rate, long-term borrowing from Lazard Brothers for the financing of Delta's Rolls Royce engines for its L-1011 fleet. This was later passed off as "dumb luck" by Oppenlander. In my view, had the decision been otherwise, i.e., to accept a rate pegged to the U.S. prime rate over the extended life of the loan, Delta's interest expense would have been as much as four or five times as great than it actually was under the Lazard loan agreement.

"Delta is basically lazy when it comes to creative financing," says a New York airline analyst, pointing out that, because of the strength of the balance sheet, Delta traditionally borrows through conventional insurance company loans and bank loans—unlike American, which has used such creative financing methods as variable rate security swap devices, municipal bond rate devices and the like.

An Atlanta banker who used to call on Delta agrees. "It was a major event when they decided to use ordinary commercial paper," he says.

The rapidly evolving availability of creative financing through the '80s seems to have escaped Delta almost entirely, either because of its siege mentality or, perhaps, the pure failure of its chief financial officer to take notice and act accordingly.

Julius Gwinn is the controller of Delta, and Frank Chew is the treasurer of Delta. Both are well educated,

personable and talented men. Yet, under Oppenlander's
tutelage, neither man was cross-pollinated into the other's
department, so that when Delta's board of directors chose a
new chief financial officer in July 1988, it was Thomas Roeck,
the former Western CFO who had joined Delta after the
merger.

The selection of Roeck may be a breath of fresh air for
Delta, a badly needed source from the outside who can help
Delta immensely in restructuring its financial thinking. It
may also be, however, that the infrastructure that Roeck
inherited is so deeply embedded in the fabric of the company that his efforts would be to no avail.

What Delta really needs is a financial ombudsman
who would give objective advice without the risk of being
charged with marching to the tune of a different drummer,
one whose advice would be heeded even if the drastic
measure of employee reductions was deemed the advice best
suited to the problem of cost.

The harsh conclusion that must be reached is that
Delta has not been under strong financial stewardship during this decade. Its management has ignored—and willfully
failed—to take advantage of the dramatic and volatile economic whirlwinds at play in the airline industry since
deregulation.

More than happy talk from overly optimistic airline
analysts and drum-beating from Delta's public relations
department are going to be needed to pull Delta's fat from
the fire. It is high time the analyst and investment community start to give Delta's management the low marks for
creativity it deserves. Certainly no actions at present would
suggest that a change in course is being contemplated.

Marketing, Marketing, Marketing

George James' earlier statement bears repeating: "One of the
most significant lessons to be learned about U.S. airline
deregulation is that marketing has become supreme in the
management structure of the airline. If the chief executive
officer is not already a marketing man, certainly the marketing voice in that company is among the strongest."[1]

Ron Allen is not a marketing man, notwithstanding his press to the contrary. If Whitley Hawkins, Delta's senior vice president—marketing, is a stronger voice in the company, it has escaped my attention during the course of writing this book. Indeed, although solicitations to shore up that assumption were actively sought from former Delta officers as well as current employees in the company, none were forthcoming.

Ruben Shohet's suggestion that Delta's marketing department should be restructured from top to bottom, while definitely radical, should be considered. At minimum, Delta should at least determine that the person who should be running the marketing department at Delta ought to be someone with a strong marketing background who already has a solid track record of success, not just a person who was charged with the sale of a product or a service.

Delta should also decentralize its marketing force and improve its staff training, particularly in the field, so that field representatives may become thoroughly familiar with computerized reservations systems. Delta's field representatives should also be given on-the-scene authority to make decisions and to help buy out a competitor's lease from a travel agent who would be willing to accept DeltaStar, the enhancement of Datas II.

It is my opinion that because of its limited capabilities, Datas II is so flawed that it is no longer a viable product in the computerized reservations systems competition. In making the recommendation in regard to DeltaStar, I rely on the advice of those within Delta who desperately believe, or want to believe, this enhancement of Datas II is or could be a powerful force in the computerized reservations systems arena. Datas II is now an outmoded product that Delta rushed to put into service at a staggering price, given its limitations, when it realized three years after the fact that the rest of the industry had automated its reservations systems.

That Delta cannot afford to languish so far behind the leading edge in technology is amply demonstrated by the fact that both American's Sabre and Texas Air's System One are used in more travel agencies in Atlanta, Delta's home town, than Datas II. By sharp contrast, in Dallas, American's home town, over 80 percent of the travel agencies use American's superior Sabre system. Of all concerns, both marketing and company-wide, rethinking its strategy in this area is perhaps most important.

Force Accountability Upon the Managers

One of the primary reasons that Delta has been unsuccessful in containing its costs over the past several years is due to the fact that there are no checks-and-balances systems throughout the company. The ultimate dispenser of purchasing authority within Delta today is the chief executive officer. No expenditure over $1,000 can be made without his express written approval. When it comes to judging whether or not a particular expenditure is in the best interest of the company, it is highly unlikely that Allen could make such decisions without relying on informed input from senior staff.

Thus, it becomes a "no brainer" for other senior officials of the company who can be persuaded by their department heads with self-serving rhetoric that particular expenditures are, in fact, not only necessary but also in the best interest of the company in general.

Delta is crippled by the commitment to its no-layoff policy and its lack of a budget process. Since effective strategic planning begins with a budget process, it would clearly behoove Delta to first examine the issue of why department heads, including those in non-profit centers within the company are not now required to produce forecasts for their departments and, second, to make such required forecasting an integral part of an overall budget process.

Complaining about projecting outside legal fees for the forthcoming fiscal year, the general counsel of a certain *Fortune* 500 Industrial company, was heard to say, "It's like trying to budget lightning, because of the unpredictability of whether or not the company will be involved in tumultuous litigation at any point in its future." True enough, but such issues force attention to that prospect, thus the budget process covers such eventualities in an anticipatory way. The same can be true of every other department within a large company.

Budgeting also has the additional therapeutic value of indicating to department heads and management in general the large percentage of the budgeted costs that salaries represent. In most departments at Delta, particularly the staff departments, the managers would be shocked to see how high the salary burden on their departments actually is.

Even a rudimentary budget process contains scenarios under which the company would respond to changes in the economic environment. For example, there is a growing consensus among economists in the United States, that the country will enter into some form of a recession the middle of 1990. If that is accurate, and assume that it is, one may well ask whether or not Delta has a contingency plan in place which it could implement in the event that airline passenger traffic should decline by a certain percentage in the next 18 months to two years. More importantly, are there other contingency plans in place if projections are not met by even wider margins?

Long-Range Planning

What should naturally flow as a result of some form of budgetary process is a more thoughtful insight into the strategic planning of the company over a longer term.

Given the historical mind set of Delta's marketing department, which argued against the acquisition of the Boeing B-727 in the early 1970s because they claimed it was too large, the predisposition to purchase the McDonnell-Douglas MD-11 is not surprising. The MD-11 appears to be a fine airplane, but it is not, by any stretch of the imagination, a B-747. It has the extended range that Delta needs to fly to the Orient, and it also offers the choice of configuration as a combination passenger/freighter aircraft. Boeing has the same with its B-747-400. The principal difference in the price of the airplanes is roughly $20 million more for the B-747-400, which also had an added chilling effect at Delta, given the fact that they tend to be frugal beyond practicality, given for example, the millions of dollars that were spent to reconfigure the L-1011 fleet for operations to the Orient.

It seems logical, therefore, that Delta opted for the McDonnell-Douglas MD-11, but it still will not be in a posture to compete effectively with other strong carriers like JAL out of Atlanta. Further, Delta ought to clarify its long-range strategies in terms of its service to some European cities.

Fortress Delta

The company should tear down the parapets surrounding its headquarters south of Atlanta and let the sunshine of the real world filter in through the tower. Because Delta has seldom innovated if it could do otherwise, it therefore remains vulnerable to the innovations of others. That other carriers are pricing discount fares to match traffic trends (although Continental doesn't always follow this script) and continue to produce, both regular and discount fares, that provide comfortable profit levels seems not to have assured Delta that innovation works. Revenues are not an issue for Delta; they are strong and getting stronger, but that does not necessarily equal profits.

One analyst gives Delta high marks for its service, but suggests that because of its "inbred management" it might be "dozing."[2] This attitude parallels those of certain other analysts, who claim that Delta is really a southern good old boys club; in some circles, the reference is to a narrow Georgia Tech alumni society. Unfortunately, these comments are generally true.

Until some catalyst is introduced which at least allows for some flexibility in Delta's promotion-from-within policy, the ability to attract top-flight managers, even from other airlines, remains slim. Remember the former Western vice president who didn't accept an offer to become an officer of Delta because he thought it was "too parochial."

Ron Allen's rise to the chairmanship of Delta is an extension of the promotion-from-within policy in its most extreme sense. Of the senior management team, only Russell Heil, who is Allen's successor as senior vice president of personnel, also a Georgia Tech graduate, and Thomas Roeck, the new chief financial officer, are younger than Allen—Roeck by only a few years.

Does this mean that Delta will have a new personnel man at its helm sometime in the first decade of 2000? Historical logic compels an affirmative answer, but the prospect is so frightening that it must be discarded.

Does Delta have somewhere a list of potential successors for Allen, assuming that he and Harris are prematurely eliminated from the scene? Does Delta's board of directors have sufficient information in its hands today to determine a qualified successor to Allen and/or Harris if either one of them leave Delta for whatever reason?

Are senior management candidates evaluated and discussed with members of the outside board of directors?

I don't know the answer to any of the foregoing questions, but one hopes contingency planning is, in fact, right up there with dividends declared and quarterly profit-and-loss statements when those who sit on Delta's board consider their responsibility to Delta shareholders.

Conclusion

Ron Allen was recently quoted as saying that he wanted Delta "...to be the most respected airline in the world."[3] This statement was made without elaboration, so it is difficult to assess the meaning or the implication Allen places on Delta's being respected.

"Successful," or perhaps "most profitable" would conjure up warm cockles in the hearts of every Delta traveler and shareholder. But "respected," on the one hand, seems to me to defy connotation in terms of its application to an airline. Respect, as in elder? Respect as in parent or spouse? My observation is that it is very difficult for an industry that has performed as poorly as the airline industry has throughout this decade to command any respect.

During the course of research for book, I interviewed a Delta captain who summed up his feelings on Delta, which are the same as mine, as follows: "Delta is living on borrowed time." Another Delta employee, a mid-level manager was less charitable. "If we don't do something drastic, the shit's gonna hit the fan within the next two years," he said. The company's management attitude is, in my opinion, bent on being so serious about the "mission" of this cult-like company that it may have lost touch with reality. Although this book is intended to provide that reality, I know that the naysayers at Delta will eschew any recommendations that I have made. So, to the ghost of Tom Beebe, and to his protege, Ron Allen, I dare you to join the real world called airline deregulation. Otherwise, you may become an insignificant footnote in an ever-changing industry.

I offer no good wishes because I have become contemptuous of what I frankly find to be contemptible: A company without accountability to its shareholders or customers and without the courage or strength to make the changes necessary to be a force of the future.

Appendix A
Chronology of Major Airline Fare Proposals

Approx. Date	Introducing Airline	Proposal	1987 Fare	Matched by	Not Matched by	General Outcome
Jan 6	UA	3-day advanced purchase	Super Coach (B Class)	AA, DL, NW, WA	TAC/CO	Withdrawn
Jan 14	TAC/CO	$10 Increase for travel after May 20 $10-$30 Increase $45 Increase 7-day advanced purchase	30-day advanced purchase Full Coach First Class QEOOP - Unrestricted — Sat night stay = 45% reduction			Sustained
Jan 30	TAC	MaxSaver Fares = 80% Discount 2-day advanced purchase Sat night stay No refund	MaxSaver	Most Majors: AA, UA, DL, NW, PA, TW, PI, WA		Offered almost systemwide
Feb 6	AA	30-day advanced purchase	MaxSaver	Most Majors	TAC/CO	Withdrawn
Feb 18	AA	After May 20: Eliminate MaxSaver and other discount fares: Increase $20	MaxSaver 14-day advanced purchase 21-day advanced purchase 30-day advanced purchase	Most Majors	TAC/CO	Withdrawn

			1987			
Approx. Date	Introducing Airline	Proposal	Fare	Matched by	Not Matched by	General Outcome
		Increase discount: to 50% from 20% Increase cancellation to 25% from 10%	7-day advanced purchase			
Mar 9	NW	Increase $20 RT ticketing after Mar 15	MaxSaver	UA*, PI, AL *not in TAC markets	TAC	Not implemented in most TAC markets
Apr 7	UA	Increase full fares	First Class OW—$15 Full/Super Coach OW—$10	TAC and most other Majors		Sustained
Apr 8	TAC/EA	New 2-day advanced purchase fare No stayover Atlanta markets	Business Savers	Delta		Sustained
Apr 21	TAC	Extend MaxSaver thru Summer Effective May 21: 7-day advanced purchase Sat night stay Non-refundable Increase $19/99 to $19/139	MaxSaver	Most Majors		Sustained

Date	Airline	Action	Description			Outcome
May 19	UA	Reduce advanced purchase to 7 days	Super Saver & F/C (30-day advanced purchase) (25% cancellation penalty)	Most Majors		Sustained
		Increase full fares	Coach RT—$20 First Class RT—$30	Most Majors	TAC	Withdrawn
June 8	TW	Fare surcharge to account for increased fuel costs	Distance surcharge $3 to $8	TAC & most other Majors		Sustained with slight modifications
Jul 13	NW	Fare increase to account for increased fuel costs (effective Aug 1)	All $2 to $8 depending on distance	Most Majors		Sustained
Aug 10	TAC/CO	Increase unrestricted Y-class	Y-Class: $2-$20 each way depending on distance B-Class unrestricted discount	Most Majors		Sustained
		Impose 3-day advanced purchase		Most Majors		Sustained
Aug 24	DL	A three-tiered structure of discount fares:	Most Restricted Discount Fares	UA, DL, NW	TAC/CO/EA	Sustained by AA, UA, DL & NW

Tier	Adv. Purch.	Penalty	% Disc
1	30	50%	60-70
2	14	25%	36-59
3	7	10%	24-55

Increase of $10-$20 OW
All effective Sep 8

1987

Approx. Date	Introducing Airline	Proposal	Fare	Matched by	Not Matched by	General Outcome
	AA	A two-tiered structure of discount fares: Tier / Adv. Purch. / Penalty 1 / 14 / 100% 2 / 7 / 50%	Most Restricted Discount Fares % Disc 60-70 40-50	UA, DL, NW	TAC/CO/EA	Sustained by AA, UA, DL & NW
		$10 above TAC 7-day advance purchase Effective Sep 15 Oct 15 (TAC Markets)	Most Restricted Discount Fares	UA, DL, NW	TAC/CO/EA	Sustained by AA, UA, DL & NW
Aug 31	TAC/EA	Reduce MaxSaver about $40 RT & extend to Caribbean (for travel Sep 9-Dec 15)	MaxSaver	UA but later withdrawn	Most Majors	Sustained by TAC/EA
Sep 7	AA	Raise OW fares $5-$15 Effective Sep 15	Unrestricted Discount Fares (Super Coach)	TAC and other Majors		Sustained
Sep 14	DL	A three-tiered structure of discount fares: Most Restricted Discount Fares Tier / Adv. Purch. / Penalty / % Disc 1 / 30 / 25% / 60-70 2 / 14 / 35% / 36-59 3 / 7 / 50% / 24-55		Other Carriers	Withdrawn	

Date	Airline	Action	Fare	Carriers Affected	TAC	Result
Oct 20	AA/DL	Increased OW fare by $10 from DFW Effective Dec 13	MaxSavers		TAC	Sustained
Oct 22	TW	Increased OW fare by $10 Effective Nov 1	All Domestic Fares	All Majors TAC: Full Fares only		Sustained
Dec 3	TW	Increased advance purchase requirement from 7 to 14 days Effective Feb 13	MaxSavers	AA/UA/PI	TAC	Not Implemented
Jan 4	TAC/CO	15%-20% reduction Reduced advance purchase from 7 to 2 days Saturday night stay No refund Good thru Feb 10	MaxSaver Fares	AA, DL, NW, AL, UA, PA		Sustained
Feb 5	AA	30-day advance purchase Effective Mar 2	MaxSaver Fares	TW, UA, DL	TAC	Not Implemented
		+$10—OW F/C +$5—OW Coach	Regular OW Fares	Most Majors		Sustained
		+$5 on RT discount fares Effective Feb 20	Ultimate Super Savers	Most Majors		Sustained
Feb 24	AL	+$10 on RT Effective Mar 2	MaxSaver	Most Majors		Sustained

Approx. Date	Introducing Airline	Proposal	1987 Fare	Matched by	Not Matched by	General Outcome
Mar 4	TAC/CO	Increase 12%-18% Effective Mar 15	First Class & Full Coach Fares	Most Majors		Sustained
		Add restrictions: 4-7 days advance purchase 25% cancellation	Capacity controlled OW Full Coach Fares (previously unrestricted)	Most Majors		Sustained
Mar 6	UA	Increase $10-$30 RT Effective May 20	MaxSaver	AA, DL, TW, PI	TAC	???
Mar 10	AA/DL	Increase advance purchase from 2 to 7 days: Effective Mar 16 7-14 days: Effective May 21	MaxSaver	Most Majors	---	Sustained
Apr 5	TAC	Reduction up to 36% Effective Apr 15-Jun 15 Travel between noon Monday & noon Tuesday Stay over Saturday	MaxSaver Fares	Most Majors in competitive markets		Sustained

Source: Airline Economics, Inc.

Abbreviations: UA—United Airlines; TAC/CO—Texas' Air Corporation/Continental Airlines; AA—American Airlines; NW—Northwest Airlines; EA—Eastern Airlines; TW—Trans World Airlines; DL—Delta Airlines.

REFERENCES

Chapter One

1 Karr, Albert R., "Scare Talk About Deregulation." *The Wall Street Journal*, May 9, 1978, p. 26.
2 *Ibid.*
3 Steven Morrison and Clifford Winston, "The Economic Effects of Airline Deregulation." Brookings Institution, 1986.
4 *Ibid.*
5 *Ibid.*
6 *Ibid.*
7 Loving, Rush, Jr., "How the Airlines Will Cope with Deregulation." *Fortune*, November 20, 1978, p. 39-41.
8 Carley, William M., "*The War Aloft*, Major Airlines Step Up Battle for Key Markets, Endanger Weak Lines." *The Wall Street Journal*, June 18, 1985, p. 6.
9 Beebe, W. T., " 'Deregulation' and the Airlines: A Plea for the Status Quo." *Finance Magazine*, November 1977, p. 3.
10 Proceedings of the Air Finance Journal Conference, April 17-19, 1988.
11 Note 7, supra.
12 Morgan, Len, "Lost Com." *Flying*, July 1987, p. 12-13.

Chapter Two

1 James, Dr. George W., *The Lessons to be Learned from*

Airline Deregulation, proceedings before The Conference on Airlines & Aircraft in the 1990s sponsored by The Association of European Airlines, June 10-11, 1987.

2 Cassidy, Arlene, "Airline Woes Catch Up With Delta." *Business Week*, November 8, 1982, p. 131.

3 Kuhn, Thomas S., *The Structure of Scientific Revolutions*, second edition, The University of Chicago Press, Chicago, 1970.

4 Note 2, supra.

5 Petzinger, Thomas, Jr., "Eastern Cutback Returns Focus To Union Fight." *The Wall Street Journal*, July 25, 1988, p. 3.

6 Note 2, supra.

7 Note 2, supra.

8 Origination and destination figures, The Boeing Company.

9 England, Thomas S., "Delta Adjusts to Flying at Less Lofty Heights." *Business Week*, January 25, 1982, p. 29-30.

10 Phillips, Carolyn and Thomas, Paulette, "Texas Air Asks Transportation Agency to Examine Rivals' Reservation Systems." *The Wall Street Journal*, August 19, 1988. p. 23.

11 Fleschner, Alan and Levere, Jane, "Newsmaker." *Travel Weekly*, September 5, 1985, p. 1.

12 Levere, Jane, *Travel Weekly*'s Economic Survey of the Travel Industry, January 30, 1985, p. 132.

13 Geewax, Marilyn, "Delta to Restructure its Discount Rates." *The Atlanta Journal Constitution*, August 22, 1987, p. 11C.

14 Geewax, Marilyn, "Consumer Group Blasts New Delta Discount-Fare Proposal." *Atlanta Journal Constitution*, August 25, 1987, p. 1-C.

15 For a complete discussion of major airline fare proposals during 1987 and 1988, see the appendix at the end of this book.

16 Banks, Howard, "Why is this Man Smiling?" *Forbes*, March 21, 1988, p. 40.

17 Rose, Robert J. and Brown, Francis C., III, "*Costly Freebies*, Frequent Flyer Plans Create a Major Mess For Airlines." *The Wall Street Journal*, February 12, 1988, p. 1.

18 Keeble, Simon, "The Cost of Flying Free." *Airline Business*, May 1, 1988, p. 46.

[19] Note 17, supra.

[20] Brummer, Alex, "Frequent Flying ... on the Ground." *Airline Business*, April 1988, p. 16.

[21] Wang, Penelope, "Accounting for an Albatross." *Forbes*, June 13, 1988, p. 62.

[22] Note 17, supra.

[23] Note 17, supra.

[24] "Industry's Triple Mileage Splurge Causes Midway First Quarter Loss." *Airline Finance News*, May 2, 1988, p. 4.

[25] "Airline Marketing." *Air Transport World*, March 1988, p. 131.

[26] Note 2, supra.

Chapter Three

[1] Carroll, Paul B., "*Computer Glitch*, Patching Up Software Occupies Programmers and Disables Systems." *The Wall Street Journal*, January 22, 1988, p. 1.

[2] Using the American Society of Travel Agents in Washington, D.C., the non-biased survey broke down travel agencies in size as follows:

Large — Those agencies with annual revenues over $5 million, which constitute 8.3 percent of all agencies in the United States;

Medium — Annual revenues between $1 and $5 million, comprising 49.5 percent of all agencies in the United States; and

Small — Those agencies with annual revenues of less than $1 million which covers 42.2 percent of all agencies in the United States.

The reason for categorizing agencies by size is to determine if attitudes and opinions vary according to the size of the agency. The agencies contacted were randomly chosen from *Travel Weekly's World Travel Directory*, a publication of Murduch Magazines, which is a geographical listing of retail and wholesale agencies in the United States and Canada.

[3] "'Halo Effect' Increases Airline Revenues of CRS Vendors." *Aviation Daily*, June 7, 1988, p. 373.

Chapter Four

[1] "Airline Consolidation—Where it Stands—What's to Come." Airline Economics, Inc., Washington, D.C., 1987, p. 2.

[2] "Yield Management." *Delta Digest*, July 1984, p. 6.

[3] In making the airline unit cost and yield differentiations, it was important to "normalize", that is, place carriers on the same comparative basis. Thus, it was important to compare carriers within similar average stage lengths, that is, average miles flown per flight, since both unit cost and yield diminished with increasing stage length. This occurs, for example, because splitting flight and ground crew costs over a longer distance provides economies of scale.

[4] Valente, Judith, "Gluttons for Punishment? Fliers Continue Using Airlines They Hate." *The Wall Street Journal*, November 19, 1987, p. 33.

[5] *Ibid.*

[6] *Ibid.*

Chapter Five

[1] Koten, John, "Pinching Pennies Keeps Profits Flying at Delta Air Lines." *The Wall Street Journal*, January 7, 1980, p. 31.

[2] The airlines compared in the Standard & Poor composite include American, Continental, Northwest, Pan American, Piedmont Aviation, TransWorld Air Lines, UAL Inc., and USAir, now the parent of Piedmont.

[3] "How the Public Companies Compare." *Georgia Trend Magazine*, July 1988, p. 100.

[4] Ticer, Scott; Payne, Seth and Toy, Stewart, "There's More Choppiness Ahead for Delta." *Business Week*, August 3, 1987, p. 30.

[5] *Ibid.*

6 *Ibid.*

7 Geewax, Marilyn, "Delta's Non-Union Workers to Get First Pay Raises in 3 Years." *The Atlanta Constitution*, July 7, 1988, p. 1B.

8 The B-scale is the lower end of a two-tier scale imposed on employees at most airlines which calls for substantially reduced pay for new entrants into the airline work force.

9 Note 7, supra.

10 Geewax, Marilyn, "Teamsters Moving to Organize Delta Baggage Handlers." *The Atlanta Constitution*, July 22, 1988, p. 1B.

11 *Ibid.*

12 "Chief Financial Officer of the Year, W. T. Beebe the Gold Winner." *Financial World*, March 15, 1978, pp. 20, 21.

13 While pilot's compensation is governed by contract and thus varies from airline to airline, some of the elements which are generally standard are such for the computation of pay and include:
Longevity — based on seniority within the airline;
Hourly rate — calculated on whether operations are during the day or at night;
Mileage pay — based on time of flight and air speed;
Gross weight pay — based on the gross weight of the aircraft being operated; and
Premiums for foreign and over water operations.

14 Since the calculation changes net earnings before taxes once the new hypothetical fuel costs are applied, the tax computation for each year for federal and state taxation are also restated.

15 Brown, Francis C., III, "Delta Air's Profit for 2nd Quarter Exceeds Estimates." *The Wall Street Journal*, January 29, 1988, p. 20.

16 Geewax, Marilyn, "Delta Stock Jumps $3.25 After Report Profits Up Sharply." *The Wall Street Journal*, January 29, 1988, p. 1B.

17 *Ibid.*

18 Williams, Winston, "Earnings Decline for Delta Air Lines." *The New York Times*, January 25, 1980, p. D4.

[19] Geewax, Marilyn, "Quarterly Profits Up 76% at Delta." *The Atlanta Journal*, July 1, 1988, p. 1B.

Chapter Six

[1] Allen, R. W. and Garrett, David C., Jr., "Report to Stockholders." *Delta Air Lines, Inc. Annual Report 1987*, July 30, 1987, p. 4.
[2] Thomas, Paulette, "Playing It Safe Has Made Delta a Winner." *The Wall Street Journal*, July 25, 1988, p. 4.
[3] *Ibid.*
[4] "Controller Strike Hurt 3rd Period, 3 Airlines Assert." *The Wall Street Journal*, October 22, 1981, p. 12.
[5] Garrett, David C., Jr., "Report to Stockholders." *Delta Air Lines, Inc. 1981 Annual Report*, August 14, 1981, p. 4.
[6] Garrett, David C., Jr., "Report to Stockholders." *Delta Air Lines, Inc. Annual Report 1983*, August 19, 1981, p. 2.
[7] Valente, Judith and Read, Eileen White, "Delta Air to Buy Up to 215 Planes of McDonnell Douglas and Boeing." *The Wall Street Journal*, September 23, 1988, p. 3.
[8] *Ibid.*

Chapter Seven

[1] James, George W., "More People, More Aircraft, More Delays." *Airline Business*, June 1987, p. 44.
[2] Sington, Philip, "Willing the End—But Not the Means." *Air Finance Journal*, November 1987, p. 26.
[3] Operations are landings or takeoffs. Enplanements on the other hand, are the number of passengers getting on and getting off airplanes at a particular point. O'Hare is still ahead in this dubious distinction.
[4] Cartwright, Dr. Phillip A., "Hartsfield International: Atlanta's Hub of Prosperity." *Georgia Trend*, October 1987. p. 11.
[5] Note 2, supra.
[6] Heffernan, Tony, "Why One Firm Rejected Atlanta." *Business Atlanta*, May 1988, p. 74.

[7] Roughton, Bert, Jr., "City Could Finance 2nd Airport Without Airline Help, Panel Says." *The Atlanta Constitution*, June 11, 1988, p. 1B.

Chapter Eight

[1] Ten years later, however, when he retired as chief executive officer in January 1980, Beebe did nothing of the sort. Like many autocrats used to complete authority, he found it hard to let go of the trappings of authority. He could be found wandering through the corridors of power at Delta until 1982, when, some say, he finally became a quarrelsome embarrassment for Garrett and was forced into complete retirement.

[2] "Chief Executive Officer of the Year." *Financial World*, March 15, 1988, p. 20.

[3] To my best recollection, within weeks after he became chief executive officer of Delta in 1970, Beebe suffered two successive massive heart attacks which resulted in bypass surgery and from which he never fully recovered. Upon his return to the office from the surgery in middle 1971 and from then on, until his departure and ultimate death, Beebe was a sick man. As I remember it, he was rarely at his desk before 10-or 10:30 a.m. and was always gone by 3-4 p.m. The day-to-day operation of the airline was, therefore, de facto, delegated primarily to Garrett. For a time, Oppenlander was misled into believing that he would be the acting CEO in Garrett's absence, but in reality it was Garrett and Allen who handled the day-to-day operations of the airline.

[4] Note 2, supra.

[5] Memory doesn't serve me well enough to explain Beebe's claim that his rug had to be cleaned once a month; I assume, however, that it was either a reference to exceptionally heavy traffic flow his office endured or to the supposedly dirty and greasy mechanics whom he probably imagined were coming into his office direct from the flight

line. In fact, Beebe was a reclusive man and had very few visitors outside of the senior executives of the company, because he was either feared or despised, or both, by most employees. In addition, he was seldom in his office.

Chapter Nine

[1] "The Acquisition and Merger of Western Airlines into Delta Air Lines." *Delta Air Lines, Inc. Annual Report 1987,* July 30, 1987, p. 5.

[2] Bean, Ed., "Delta Air Names Allen to Its Top Posts to Succeed Retiring Chairman Garrett." *Wall Street Journal,* July 24, 1987, p. 21.

[3] *Ibid.*

[4] Deans, Bob, "Delta Flying Smoothly into Rough Skies." *Atlanta Journal Constitution,* July 12, 1987, p. 1A.

[5] "Delta's Record for Late Flights Among Worst in September." *The Atlanta Journal,* November 10, 1987, p. 1A.

[6] Ewing, T. Hunter, Letter to the Editor, *The Atlanta Journal,* November 19, 1987.

[7] Note 5, supra.

[8] Witkin, Richard, "F.A.A. Says Delta Had Poor Policies on Crew Training." *The New York Times,* September 19, 1987, p. 1.

[9] Parker, Laura, "FAA Criticizes Delta Pilots For Lapses in Crew Discipline." *The Washington Post,* September 19, 1987, p. 1A.

[10] *Ibid.*

[11] Note 9, supra.

[12] Note 8, surpa.

[13] Johnson, Terry E., with Smith, Vern E., "What's Wrong With Delta?" *Newsweek,* July 27, 1987, p. 25.

Chapter Ten

[1] James, George W., "The Lessons to be Learned from Air-

line Deregulation." Remarks before The Conference on Airlines & Aircraft in the 1990s, sponsored by The Association of European Airlines, June 10-11, 1987, p. 4.

[2] Neidl, Ray, "How a Junk Bond Analyst Rates the Airlines." *Air Transport World*, September 1988, p. 62.

[3] Ticer, Scott, "Why the Folks at Delta are Walking on Air." *Business Week*, August 1, 1988, p. 92-93.